WEXFORD

WEXFORD
A History, A Tour
and A Miscellany

NICKY ROSSITER

NONSUCH

First published 2005

Nonsuch Publishing
73 Lower Leeson Street,
Dublin 2
Ireland
www.nonsuch-publishing.com

A catalogue record for this book is available from the National Library.

ISBN 1 84588 528 7

Typesetting and origination by Nonsuch Publishing Limited
Printed in Great Britain

CONTENTS

Acknowledgements   7

Introduction   9

THE HISTORY OF WEXFORD   11
Chapter One:
From Legend to the Normans   11
Chapter Two:
Charter, Cromwell and 1798   17
Chapter Three:
The Nineteenth Century and The 1911 Lockout   27
Chapter Four:
The First World War, The Civil War and The Second World War   41
Chapter Five:
Into the Modern Era   51

THE MISCELLANY   57

A TOUR - WALKS INTO OUR PAST   103

Bibliography   155

Biography:

Nicky Rossiter was born and reared in Wexford. He has written extensively on the town and social history as well as folk music. He was co-author and author of a number of books on Wexford. He has contributed to *The Journal of the Wexford Historical Society*, *Sunday Miscellany* (on RTE), *Ireland's Own*, *Irish Music Magazine*, *The Bridge*, national and local publications. He researches, writes, produces and presents a series of programmes on local history and folk music on South East Radio and runs a website devoted to Wexford history. He lives 'over the water' at Screen with his wife Anne, back in the parish of his ancestors.

To Anne

The author pictured beside a plaque to the people involved in the Lockout of 1911.

He provided the inscription. (Paddy Donovan collection)

ACKNOWLEDGEMENTS

THE COMPILATION OF A BOOK like this can only be accomplished with the goodwill and assistance of many people. Thanking them is a dangerous task because I am bound to omit someone and if this happens I apologize most profusely.

Without my wife Anne none of the books or projects I have undertaken in recent years would have been possible. The history bug bit in the 1980s and Tomas Hayes, Kevin Hurley and Willie Roche nurtured its bite. Together we produced some very popular publications. Because history doesn't change, some of the material here will draw on the texts of those and of other books that I wrote alone but it has been revised and updated in the light of new research.

Photographs are the lifeblood of most local history books and where possible I have acknowledged the donors in the captions. With the collection of photos I have amassed for research purposes some have origins lost in the mist of time and memory. If I reproduced something you gave me without acknowledgement, please forgive me, let me know and I will amend it in any future edition. We have tried to use the best quality photographs possible but on occasion we have used less than perfect old images where we consider the content superior to quality.

I thank Paddy Donovan, Tomas Hayes, Kevin Hurley, Willie Roche, Celestine Rafferty, The National Library of Ireland, Wexford County Library Service, Tom Mooney (the Echo Group), John Rossiter, the late Wally Doyle and others for photographs, information, facts and any other assistance given over the years this book was in gestation.

Thanks to Eoin Purcell of Nonsuch Publishing for having faith in the project.

INTRODUCTION

WELCOME TO MY VIEW OF Wexford. Almost twenty years ago I was part of a group that produced a book on the history of the town. Much has changed in those two decades and the thirst for information on our past has grown. The increase in the popularity of history at international, national and local level has been phenomenal. This book will give the resident and the visitor a broad as well as an intimate picture of the town or 'ancient and historic borough' of Wexford as our local politicians delight in calling it. I hope you will find the stories interesting, amusing, revealing and educational.

The book is divided into three sections:

The history by its very nature is unchanging and will be familiar in many places but I have used the most recent findings to expand and explain features of our past.

The Miscellany section is a potpourri of our heritage from centuries ago to the relatively recent past. It gives you a chance to sample the unique flavour of Wexford. Here you will find characters, histories of places and events that could not fit comfortably into either of the other sections. It can be read straight through or dipped into at leisure.

The tour is a marathon but you are welcome to take it in stages. In fact by using a range of photographs I hope that you could tour the town from your armchair although walking it would be healthier and more fulfilling.

Throughout the book I have included photographs, sketches and old advertisements. The majority will not have been published before but some old favourites are reproduced, as they are essential to your enjoyment. I hope you enjoy this look at our heritage and history. I firmly consider history to be a living thing and I would be delighted with your feedback, your memories and your photographs for another publication at a later date.

This is Menapia, Loch gCarman, Weisfiord, Wexford.

Nicky Rossiter
stories@iol.ie

CHAPTER ONE

FROM LEGEND TO THE NORMANS

THE LEGEND:

Once upon a time there lived a great queen. Her prize possession was a golden crown. A young man named Carman coveted this treasure and stole it from the queen. He travelled to the southeast corner of Ireland pursued by the queen's enchantress.

On finding the robber this enchantress used her magical power to send forth a great flood. Carman was caught in the torrent and drowned. The crown was retrieved and given back to the queen. So great was the torrent of water that when it eventually settled it formed a great expanse of mudflats and small islands where once a river valley had been. In legend this water was named The Lake of Garman or in Irish Loch gCarman.

THE BEGINNING:

Looking at the topography of the area of Wexford we see that it may have been a pleasant and viable area of settlement for peoples arriving by land, by coastal navigation or from the Welsh coast.

Two fresh water rivers, later called The Bishopswater and Peter, flowing into the harbour with forested margins would have provided the basic requirements to sustain settlement. The bay was very different from that viewed by current visitors. Today Wexford has encroached at least 200 metres into the harbour through land reclamation and quay development. In addition, the reclamation of the sloblands opposite the quays incorporated a number of islands.

This was not a paradise island. Life was a constant struggle. Clothing would have been made from skins of slain animals. Wild animals provided meat while berries and wild fruits together with wild honey supplemented the meagre produce of the initial primitive farming using 'slash and burn' clearance of the forests. Wexford also had the advantage of produce from the harbour in the form of fish, shellfish and wild fowl. The

This is a map of Wexford Haven prior to reclamation. Begerin had been renamed Great Island since the days of Saint Ibar.

This plaque showing Dermot McMurrough, Henry 11 and Robert Fitzstephen stood for many years at Gibson's Lane or Royal Street as it may have been called.
(Rossiter Collection)

12

settlement must have expanded and trade established. The primary settlement at Wexford appears to have been in the Selskar area at the north end of the present Main Street.

MENAPIA:

Ptolemy's map, possibly the first detailed representation of Ireland in cartography, was sketched around the year AD150. It is not really a map as we are familiar with. It was based on reports of numerous sailors returning to Egypt. Ireland is named as Ivernia, which may have given rise to its later title of Hibernia.

We must use some detective work to establish the locations. Sacred Cape refers to Carnsore Point. Brigos may be the River Barrow. Madonnas as the major river entering the sea at the Southeast corner must represent the present Slaney and the settlement at its mouth named Menapia is the earliest representation of Wexford town. Menapia is derived from the Menapii tribe.

CHRISTIANITY:

Ibar was a man of noble birth and is said to have been one of the first Irish born bishops of the Christian Church. Wexford tradition held that Ibar introduced the faith here before the arrival of Saint Patrick. A more likely explanation is that both, and perhaps other missionaries, arrived in Ireland at about the same time and worked independently. Imagine one man trying to convert a country today even with modern media and refer that to an island with little in the way of roads or communications or even cohesive society and you see the logic of this.

Ibar's name is to be found throughout the county - as a relatively popular Christian name for boys, in the Latin, Iberius, as a church name and in older documents, as Iver or Ivory, as parish names. The most common usage today is as the name of the main cemetery for the town. Ibar arrived in Wexford from Meath and established a school on Begerin, an island in the harbour. We do not know when Ibar was born or died but we can assume the latter was around the year AD 500 and 23 April is classed as his feast day. In the life of St Abban there is mention of him being buried on Begerin and of miracles occurring. In the Stowe Missal, compiled around the ninth century there is an invocation– 'I honour Bishop Ibar who heals'.

Giraldus Cambrensis, writing in the Twelfth century tells a tale of Ibar being plagued by rats on his island. They were eating his holy books and in a rage he banished all vermin from the region. A comparison with Patrick and the snakes is interesting.

The monastic settlement at Begerin continued long after the death of Ibar and Christianity was firmly established in Wexford. In AD 819 there were reports of relics being removed because the Norsemen had attacked the island of Begerin.

VIKINGS:

The stories of Viking raids are the stuff of adventure and legend. Such raids were common for decades on coastal settlements in Ireland, The British Isles and Europe. The raids gradually developed into settlement. By the year 892 the Norsemen had settled and were referring to the harbour as Weisfiord. Outside the Norse Stockade the old Celtic settlement continued to grow around the ferry point near Selskar.

The Norsemen had timber from the forests for shipbuilding and repairs, fish from harbour waters and game from the woods. There was shelter from the winter gales in the broad haven. The original settlement is believed to have been around the mouth of the present Bishopswater River in the south end of the town. They built their houses and erected defenses of ditches and wooden palisades. The extent of the Norse town was earlier calculated from the parishes whose names and boundaries are still in existence but no longer used. Saint Michael's of Feagh on the height above their settlement bears a dedication to Michael the Archangel, a patron saint of the Norsemen. Another church of the area was St Doologues or Olaves, a Danish name. There was also the Holy Trinity Church, suggesting a Norse foundation as Christ Church in Norse Dublin was also dedicated to the Holy Trinity.

More recent research by Dr. Billy Colfer indicates that the Norse town was much larger. It is now believed to have extended as far as the Bullring area although that feature did not exist at the time. This allows it to incorporate the two archaeological sites at Bride Street and Oyster Lane. His research indicates that the old settlement and the Norse town almost met at that point with a 'Common Plain' as the Bullring was known, between them.

The houses were probably made of mud-plastered wattle. The roof was of thatch with a central aperture to release the smoke. The houses were susceptible to fires and to collapse, in which case a replacement was built on the same site. Excavations in the South Main Street area of Wexford referred to above late in the twentieth century revealed a number of such houses and provide valuable evidence of our Norse past. Houses were built close together and had small gardens for the growing of staple foods. Pigs were reared in the muddy streets. Dogs and cats were kept as working pets, as Saint Ibar had not succeeded in removing the vermin.

In Norse Wexford the current Main Street was a narrow trail running along the edge of the harbour. Norse towns like Wexford usually paid tribute to local chieftains in order to sustain a peaceful existence. Towns with large fleets hired out their ships in times of war and there is a record of the fleets of Dublin, Waterford and Wexford assisting King Henry II against the Welsh. At the battle of Clontarf in 1014 the natives of Wexford were part of the force of Leinstermen who fought against Brian Boru.

NORMAN INVASION:

A large army approached Wexford in May 1169. A force from the town went to meet them. Instead of finding an army of 'Kerns' or hired soldiers armed with spears and battle-axes, they intercepted a superior force. This was a well-disciplined Norman army invited to Ireland by Dermot McMurrough. It was an army of great battle experience, helmeted and clad in chain mail. These professional soldiers were flanked by troops of archers with their longbows. The Wexford men retreated to the walled town, burning houses on the outskirts as they went, depriving the enemy of shelter. Giraldus Cambrensis has left us an account of the ensuing battle.

The Norman army approached the town. They crossed marshland at the present King Street and the river that we know as the Bishopswater. They took the high ground where Carrigeen is situated today. Robert Fitzstephen deployed his archers, with a commanding view of the town's defenses. Under a hail of arrows, the Normans rushed forward and began to fill parts of the defensive ditch, then withdrew. This process was repeated a number of times, until a path to the walls was constructed. Another assault saw them begin to scale the walls. The inhabitants repulsed the attackers with rocks and timbers hurled from the ramparts. A group of Norman soldiers set fire to the boats moored at a nearby beach. This incident may have provided the inspiration for Wexford's later town crest of three burning ships. Eighteen Normans and three townsmen died in the battle according to Giraldus.

The Norman troops assembled for Mass next morning. Wexford faced a siege, a form of warfare that basically starving the enemy into submission. It proved highly effective throughout Europe. This indicates that all of Wexford's boats had been destroyed, otherwise supplies could have been brought into the besieged town from the other side of the harbour. The townspeople decided to sue for peace. Two bishops who were resident in Wexford at the time of the attack carried on negotiations. Wexford surrendered.

The town walls were rebuilt, strengthened and extended. This was undertaken by order of King Henry II. He arrived in town from Dublin in March 1172. Being the season of Lent, much of his time was spent in prayer and fasting in one of the town's churches. A tradition refers to Selskar Abbey, but this is unlikely as its foundation by Alexander Roche dates from the Third Crusade in the reign of Richard the Lionheart.

In a chronicle dated 1592, there is a reference to Royal Street in St Mary's Parish. This may have been named to commemorate King Henry residing there, probably in the house of the Bishop of Ferns on his visit in 1172 and may refer to Peter Street. Henry visited Wexford to formally take possession of the town and to demonstrate his supreme power. On 17 April 1172, Easter Monday, Henry II proceeded via today's Peter Street to the ship wharf near the present Crescent and left for Wales.

Town walls were defensive but they also marked boundaries. They marked the border between residents and non-residents, between those entitled to town privileges and those not so entitled. Wexford's six town gates were closed from sunset to sunrise. The admission of traders, travellers, mendicants and vagrants was controlled. Tolls were collected on goods brought into town for sale. Within the walls of Wexford town life became more organised and formal. Laws designated the marketplaces. Corn and potatoes were sold at Cornmarket. All meat was sold in the 'Shambles' or Meat Market at the Bull Ring. Wexford was part of the Norman world.

This square tower is at Mallin Street.

(Rossiter Collection)

CHAPTER TWO

CHARTER, CROMWELL AND 1798

CHARTER:

The 1317 Charter granted to Wexford by Aymer de Valence, Earl of Pembroke, outlined the regulations governing the town. It referred to the appointment of burgesses from among whom a mayor and bailiffs were chosen. The Merchants Guild was established in Wexford by the charter.

Wexford in the 1300s had streets and laneways harbouring dunghills and pigsties, which were said to infect the air and 'produce fevers, pestilence and death.' Fire was such a danger that any person found guilty of causing a fire was fined one hundred shillings and anyone unable to pay could be thrown into the flames.

There was in Wexford a tradition of pilgrimage to the tomb of Friar John, where the sick were cured and the dead revived. In 1348 the people flocked to the tomb to pray for deliverance from the Black Death as it raged across Europe.

In 1410, the Charter of Aymer de Valence was confirmed and enlarged by King Henry IV. From then a mayor and bailiffs were chosen annually and a mayor's court was held in the Tholsel. The charter of 1410 gave the mayor the power to call men to arms and also to set a fair price for goods sold in the Market Place.

THE REFORMATION:

The sixteenth century brought religious upheaval to Europe as the Catholic Church split. In January 1539, George Browne, Protestant Archbishop of Dublin, visited Wexford preaching Royal Supremacy in church matters. Suppression of the Catholic religion was inevitable. Rather than acknowledge the claims of the king by voluntarily surrendering their property, the friars who had been the primary religious force in Wexford quietly disappeared from public view. They lived in the homes of Wexford's faithful and ministered to their flock in secret.

When Queen Mary succeeded to the English throne in 1553 there was a relaxation

This is the crest and town
motto for Wexford.

of religious persecution. The Wexford friars took possession of their friary once more, with the help of Paul Turner who held a lease on the property. Turner bequeathed the lands in trust for them in his will of February 1557. The reign of Queen Mary was short as was the return of the friars to their church, and once again they went into hiding. In a time of further religious persecution the Wexford Friars celebrated Mass daily for the people of the town in the ruined churches or in Mass Houses located in the town.

Around 1615 they secured a permanent house in High Street and later in 1620, had a small thatched chapel in Archer's Lane, which connected Main Street to High Street.

In 1609, James I granted a charter to Wexford. It permitted the introduction of local laws and byelaws for the benefit of the inhabitants and allowed the governing body of 24 burgesses to introduce new guilds.

THE COAT OF ARMS
The earliest mention Wexford's Coat of Arms was in 1618. On the sketch of the crest according to the History of Wexford Town and County by Philip Herbert Hore, when Sir Daniel Molyneux, Ulster King of Arms visited the town he returned the arms of the town as a ship in flames with the motto, 'Per aquam et ignem. The motto translates as "through fire and water". This is corroborated by a document in the British Museum. A small sketch shows at the top the words 'The Towne of Vexfort' and below a small brig surrounded by flames. It would later show three ships.

SEVENTEENTH CENTURY:
In 1621 a charter or privilege granted to the butchers of Wexford required the said butchers to provide, twice yearly on 24 August and 21 November, 'a bull to be baited by dogs'. The hide of the animal was presented to the Mayor and the carcass used to feed the poor. The custom lasted until 1770 and the baiting took place in the Bullring, hence the name.

Richard Wadding was elected to Parliament for Wexford in 1613. Mr. Wadding never sat in Parliament, as he refused to swear the Oath of Supremacy. This refusal indicated a growing attitude of the time. A meeting held outside the town at the hill of Carrig, in October 1641, attended by many of the gentry of the area may be seen as the first steps towards rebellion. The official date of Wexford in rebellion is 21 December, 1641.

It was precipitated by land plantation. Families whose lands had been confiscated began to agitate against the crown and attacks were made on those farming the confiscated land.

The rebel force in Wexford in 1641 was calculated as 800. The defenses were strengthened and all buildings within eight feet of the town wall were evacuated. The harbour was blockaded with timber beams and chains. A ship called *The Hopewell* was lured to the Saltee Islands and wrecked. Its guns were brought to Wexford.

In January 1642 more than sixty Protestants attempted to flee the town by boat. It foundered just outside the bay and all but one was lost. In the summer of 1642 a declaration was made, that 'no English or Protestant man, woman, child, beast or dog should remain, and all the bibles found belonging to those people in Wexford were burned.'

The Spanish flag was paraded through the streets to great cheering. The flag also flew from the Wexford Castle. Wexford Harbour was busy with the ships of the Navy of the Confederation of Kilkenny. They constantly harassed the English fleets and many vessels captured were brought to Wexford town and sold to local businessmen. Captured Confederate sailors were tied back to back and thrown into the sea, a common punishment meted out to pirates. This enraged the Wexford people and Jasper Bolan, Mayor, in a letter to parliament, threatening to execute one hundred and sixty-eight prisoners held in Wexford if the practice did not cease.

On Easter Saturday 1647, Cardinal Rinucinni, the Papal Envoy, arrived at Wexford by river from Enniscorthy. He was welcomed with cannon salutes from the town walls and ships in the harbour. He was guest of honour at a reception hosted by the Corporation. A liturgical reception took place in St Peter's Church. On leaving Wexford on the following Wednesday he described his reception as 'the greatest manifestation of loyalty to Rome he had experienced in Ireland.' The rebellion continued.

In England, King Charles I was executed and Oliver Cromwell took on the title of Lord Protector, and in 1649 began a campaign against the rebels in Ireland.

CROMWELL:

On Tuesday 2 October 1649, seven thousand foot soldiers and two thousand cavalry set up camp at present day Carcur near Wexford. Twenty ships lay offshore outside the harbour protected by the Fort at Rosslare. Oliver Cromwell was at Wexford.

A small force of dragoons captured the fort at Rosslare despite its seven cannon and an armed frigate in attendance. Artillery was landed and taken to the area now called 'The Rocks'. This area is located at the rear of the present Faythe houses. The town was surrounded. Negotiations began between Cromwell and Colonel David Sinnott, Governor of the town. Letters passed between the two parties over a number of days, during which some reinforcements were landed in the town from the Ferrybank side of the Slaney.

A week after arriving at Wexford, on 9 October, Cromwell's troops took up a new position beside the cannon battery at Trespan Rock. The castle in today's Barrack Street then stood just outside the town wall. Were it to be captured the town would fall. On

11 October, the battery at Trespan opened fire on the Castle. A number of breaches were made. The defenders were steadfast despite the bombardment. However, Colonel Sinnott renewed negotiations. One of Sinnott's envoys was James Stafford, governor of the Castle. Knowing the damage already inflicted on the castle he delivered it to Cromwell in return for the lives of himself and his men. Cromwell agreed.

The attacking army on taking the castle fired down into the town. The defenders knew it was lost and fled. The Cromwellian army scaled the walls and opened the Castle Gate of Wexford town. The townspeople ran in terror before the attackers. Despite heavy fighting there were few casualties among the attackers. Cromwell claimed to have lost only five men in the assault.

Reports of between fifteen hundred to two thousand townspeople dying by the sword or by drowning while trying to flee would appear to be an exaggeration. In 1840 the town only would only boast a population of around 3,000. From Thursday 11 October 1649, stories were widespread of shots deflected by crucifixes, blood indelibly staining the killers' hands and Puritan soldiers converting to Catholicism.

In Mayglass, some miles from Wexford town, it was said that a beautiful woman ascended to the sky from the direction of the town on that fateful day. The story of the massacre of 200 women huddled around 'the market cross' most likely relates to people killed in the market place, at a crossroads, rather than to a crucifix. The unearthing of human remains in the Bullring area in later years gives some credence to the story. The first written account did not appear until 1763.

Cromwell remained in Wexford until 17 October at Kenny's Hall (now incorporated into 'Penney's' at South Main Street). Wexford was a town of ruined buildings, desecrated churches and a very small population. Tradition has it that only twenty Catholics spent Christmas in Wexford in 1649. Within a few months people began to return from the countryside, by permission of the garrison commander Colonel Cooke.

The return was encouraged because the town needed to be rebuilt in order to attract settlers. Those who returned lived as tenants in homes they once owned. Many people are said to have been shipped to Barbados from Kaat Quay near the present the Westgate.

In 1653 a decree banished all priests from the country. A bounty of five pounds was put on clerics, the same amount as could be claimed for a wolf, an animal still plentiful in the woods at the time.

An interesting set of statistics from 1659 records that: 'The town was divided into wards: East, West, South and North. The suburbs were Faigh (The Faythe), Bridstreete (Bride Street), St John Streete (John Street), Weststreete (Westgate) and Maudlintown.'

Bride Street is classed as a suburb.

'The families included 14 Murphys, 11 Synotts (Sinnotts), 7 Welshes (Walshes), 13 Codds, 6 Doyles, 6 Whites, 5 Connors, 5 Furlongs, 5 Redmonds and 5 Devereuxes.'

A law passed in 1659 prohibited Irish and English in Ireland being granted a license to sell strong drink to be consumed indoors. Rather than curbing drinking the attempt to abolish inns or alehouses was a political ideal to get rid of buildings where plots and conspiracy could thrive.

By 1674 things were not ideal but they had improved. Dr. Luke Wadding, Bishop of Ferns, started building a chapel on the west side of High Street. Reports are that it was complete with rails, confessional and a pulpit. It cost £53 14s. 9d and could accommodate 40 people. The chapel served for about 10 years before falling into disrepair. Because it was within the walled town, permission to repair it was required but was refused.

In 1687 James II was granted a charter to Wexford. It had early references to a Town Clerk and Aldermen. It also granted permission for a mayoral seal. James fled to France after his defeat at the Boyne and the Charter was annulled. Wexford reverted to the 1609 Charter that would remain in force until 1840.

Thomas Knox, a descendant of John Knox, the religious reformer, became Governor of Wexford in 1690. Knox was instrumental in the settlement of some Huguenots, a French Protestant group, in the Faythe area of Wexford.

INSURRECTION 1798:

The United Irishmen were founded with a desire for a republic based on liberty and equality for all. In the words of its own manifesto, it was:

'A brotherhood of affection, a communion of right, and a union of power among Irishmen of every religious persuasion . . . on the principles of civil, political and religious liberty.'

In County Wexford Catholic and Protestant joined together and vowed to resist the payment of tithes (taxes). Such groupings grew and convened mostly at churches and chapels at times of religious services. At such gatherings others were urged to resist. The royal magistrates were infuriated and took to raiding such gatherings, accompanied by troops.

Sixteen men were arrested near Bunclody and brought to Enniscorthy. With bad feelings rising in the region and it was decided that 14 of them should be released on bail. Because two of the group had been armed when taken they were transferred to the larger county gaol at Wexford town. Neighbours of the men set out for Wexford town. On the road to the town many others joined this throng. Some felt a sense of injustice. The protestors forced others along. A messenger was sent ahead, to demand the release of the prisoners. No such release would be contemplated.

Fifty soldiers, under the command of Major Charles Vallotin, a veteran of the war in Spain, along with three magistrates went to meet them at the present Upper John Street.

At Wygram, on the edge of town Vallotin went forward alone to reason with the crowd. John Moore spoke for the countrymen. During the talks Vallotin noticed a fellow officer held prisoner by the crowd. In his fury he thrust his sword into Moore. Moore fell but as he did, he struck his assailant with a scythe. The militia opened fire on the crowd, who ran panic stricken, in all directions.

Captain Boyd returning with his troop from Taghmon, and seeing the commotion, laid an ambush at Bettyville and further decimated the fleeing rebels. As dusk fell on the 11 July 1793, eleven men lay dead at John Street. These were left on public view for some time as an example to others. Among the dead were four Protestants and also an innocent cobbler from the town, who had been forced to join the crowd. Vallotin died of his wound. The Corporation erected a large pinnacle monument to his memory near the site of the battle at Wygram, which still stands. John Moore also died of his wounds.

Eight men were discovered hiding in a hayloft on the day. One died of his wounds, two became informers and five were tried, convicted and executed on 26 July at Windmills Hill. The events of that July day caused great fear and anxiety in the town and over the coming years tensions seldom eased. A fall in barley prices and new

21

Vallotin Monument (Rossiter Collection)

malting legislation in 1797 caused unemployment and financial distress throughout Britain and Ireland. The 'Peep 0' Day Boys' and the 'Orangemen' grew in number and in reputation. Although neither of the groups was strong in Wexford at the time, the fears of the people mounted. Arms, particularly pikes were clandestinely manufactured. The pike was a simple but ingenious weapon. Its hook was used to wrench the reins of cavalrymen to de-horse them while the spear like point was used to stab adversaries.

Large areas of the country were placed under what amounted to martial law early in 1798. The army was placed 'at free quarters', meaning that soldiers had authority to commandeer homes and demand that the local population feed them and care for their needs. By 30 March 1798, the whole of Ireland was under martial law.

The North Cork Militia, commanded by Lord Kingsborough, was stationed in County Wexford. The 'pitch cap' made its appearance in Wexford in the spring of that year. This instrument of torture consisted of a cap of coarse linen or strong brown paper smeared with hot pitch. It was placed on the victim's head with easily imagined results. Anyone suspected of sympathizing with the United Irishmen was liable for such treatment.

Landlords tried to defuse the situation. They arranged the surrender of arms held by the people and issued them with certificates of character. It was hoped that such surrenders would save them from the military. On Whit Sunday, 27 May 1798, Bagenal Harvey of Bargy Castle entered Wexford town in order to deliver arms so collected for safekeeping by the military. He was arrested by Captain Boyd and thrown into gaol. Mr. Turner arrived in town later with news of people burning and plundering homes in the countryside. The rebellion of 1798 had started.

A company of North Cork Militia comprising of 109 infantry and 19 yeomen cavalry set out from Wexford to quell the rebels at Oulart. Only four men returned to the town. Tension rose in Wexford. Colleagues of the slain soldiers sought revenge. Attempts were made to kill the prisoners held in the town but the gaoler armed them and a number of assaults were repulsed.

Enniscorthy fell to the rebels and refugees fled to Wexford with tales of slaughter.

Wexford approaches were barricaded. The old town gates were hastily re-erected and cannon placed in the streets. On the 29 May, 200 Donegal Militia with one six-pounder arrived from Duncannon, having marched all night. The Taghmon Cavalry also arrived on the same day. With fear of the town being burned, all fires were ordered to be extinguished, even bakers ovens. All thatch was stripped from the houses in the town. The forces in Wexford town were: 300 Cork Militia, 200 Donegal Militia, five troops of volunteer yeomen, five troops of cavalry and 200 armed civilian, making a total of 1,200 men. Harvey, Colclough and Fitzgerald were asked to use their influence with the rebels. It was arranged that the men be released on bail to go to the rebel camp that was located at the Three Rocks.

The rebels had not contemplated taking on the crown forces. Their successes were surprising and they had no plans for consolidating their position. They were preparing to go back to their homes when Colclough and Fitzgerald arrived at the camp. Suddenly they believed that Wexford could be taken. Colclough, still on horseback, addressed the town's officials at the Bullring with this news. Streets were quickly deserted. Shops

The toll house at the Ferrybank side of the old 1794 Oak Bridge.

23

and lower windows of houses were boarded up, and passage on sailing vessels was at a premium. The town prepared for an attack.

Next morning the tollhouse on the eastern end of the bridge at Ferrybank was seen to be in flames. The fire was extinguished and only slight damage had been caused to the bridge. But the very fact that the bridge was attacked caused panic in the town.

Soldiers discarded uniforms and weapons into the harbour. They dressed in civilian clothes and tried to blend into the population. A yeoman, named Doyle was to deliver a letter from Harvey to the rebel camp. When it was revealed that he was a Catholic, he was not trusted and the Richards brothers were sent instead. At this time many professional soldiers were deserting. The yeomen and armed civilians were left alone. The crowds at Ferrybank boarded up the burned part of the bridge and crossed into town.

George Taylor printed all proclamations and edicts of the rebel forces. It is said a sign 'printer to the republic' was displayed in his Wexford shop. The garrison of the town, depleted by fleeing professional soldiers surrendered. Prisoners were released from the gaols. Bagenal Harvey became commander. The town was decorated with green boughs.

As rebels from Three Rocks entered town the men wanted to burn the town. There was no co-ordination between the rebels and the people who came across the bridge and in this confusion many soldiers in disguise escaped.

The 30 May 1798 was a quiet night but with daybreak came plunder and chaos on the crowded streets. The inhabitants asked the rebel forces to leave the town in peace and this they did. They camped at the Windmills Hill and fields along the present Belvedere Road before marching away to Gorey and other parts. People came from the countryside and paraded through Wexford with pitchforks, scythes and other 'weapons' before returning home. Forges in town and country were manufacturing pikes, including a vast open-air forge at the Bullring. A person was not considered dressed unless armed and wearing a hat decorated with a cockade or a green band.

Four armed oyster boats patrolled the outer harbour, each with a crew of twenty-five men. The Fort at Rosslare had three old cannon. Four sloops were placed, ready to be scuttled, in order to protect the harbour. The patrol boats seized provisions from ships to feed the town. Country people were too afraid to come to markets and supplies were dwindling. Food that was available was sold for coin money only. Bank notes were useless and went to light pipes or fires.

On 2 June, 1798, the patrol boats captured a ship in the outer harbour. On board were three officers, including Lord Kingsborough. He was brought ashore and lodged at Captain Keogh's house. The people demanded that this commander of the North Cork Militia be imprisoned. The gaol was full so he was put under guard at a house in the Bullring, now The Cape Bar.

Thomas Dixon, a sea captain and porterhouse owner now decided to 'settle old scores'. His relative, Father Dixon, was sentenced to deportation on the word of an informer just before the rising. Dixon now had this man named Murphy taken to the Bullring. There he is said to have forced three revenue officers, also prisoners, to execute him by firing squad and throw his body into the Slaney.

The tide was turning against the rebels throughout the county. They began to fall back on Wexford. The town was soon crowded with insurgents. The overcrowded conditions of the gaol, combined with the unusually warm weather of that summer, caused fears of a fever epidemic. A suggestion that the Protestant Church be used as a prison to ease the situation was over-ruled by a majority of Catholics who saw such action as disrespectful to the Protestant religion.

Dixon's personal vendettas continued. He took eighteen men from the gaol at Stonebridge to a public billiard room on Custom House Quay. There they were convicted on the word of the informers and taken to the bridge. People pleading on their behalf for past good deeds saved some. The rest died by the gun or the pike. Their bodies were thrown into the river. More prisoners were then called from their places of confinement. Dixon was determined to kill all the captives.

Fr. Corrin arrived back in Wexford from duties as Parish Priest and rushed to the scene of slaughter. He fell to his knees and prayed that God would show the same mercy to the people as they showed to the prisoners. His pleas saved many lives. Others were saved by the intervention of Esmonde Kyan and by Edward Roche who came and ordered the ringleaders to march out to the Three Rocks. On 20 June 1798, 35 men were killed at the bridge and another person at the gaol.

By now government forces were drawing closer to the town. It was agreed that surrender was the only way to save further loss of life. Captain Keogh presented his sword to Lord Kingsborough as a symbol of Wexford's surrender. General Moore and his troops approached the town. All green emblems disappeared. Moore's troops were bent on the destruction of Wexford. They were kept outside the town and camped at Windmills Hill, overlooking the streets and the harbour. Moore demanded that the leaders of the rebellion be handed over to him. He disregarded Kingsborough's acceptance of the surrender.

Moore's army was brutal in victory. The bodies of those already dead were mutilated. The bridge again became a place of death. The rebels were hoisted up and hanged from an ornamental arch. Then they were stripped and mutilated and cast into the river. Some were beheaded and their heads placed on spikes above the courthouse in the Bullring One such victim was John Kelly, famed in song as 'Kelly the Boy from Killanne'. He was taken to the place of execution on a cart and beheaded. He had been wounded at New Ross. His body was thrown into the Slaney and his head used as a football in a gruesome game along the Custom House Quay. So ended an episode of Wexford history, much celebrated in song and story, which was marked by cruelty on both sides.

An interesting coincidence is that John Moore was the name of the man who killed Vallotin and John Moore was the name of the commander who took Wexford five years later. Similarly many of those executed on Wexford Bridge had been shareholders and subscribers for its construction four years earlier.

CHAPTER THREE

THE NINETEENTH CENTURY AND THE 1911 LOCKOUT

THE NINETEENTH CENTURY:

In 1805 the old courthouse at The Bullring was demolished. The building had stood beside the present National Irish Bank premises at The Bullring but on the present roadway. It faced 'The Gut' or narrow entrance to Cornmarket from the Bullring across a narrow lane. The demolition was undertaken in order to open up the Main Street and Bullring. It was also to accommodate the mail coach with its team of four horses. An interesting feature that again indicates this as the intersection of old and new Wexford is the street alignment. The old Foreshore Street simply did not meet any of the Norse town street head on. Another anomaly is that for years we talked about our narrow Viking streets and referred to the fact that at the old White's Hotel you could 'shake hands with a friend standing on the opposite footpath'. But in truth this was not part of Viking Wexford.

Wexford was in a period of economic expansion in the early nineteenth century. The Corporation bought most of the former shambles or meat market from Mr. Sparrow and built a Tholsel. This housed the Corporation offices and a 'Court of Conscience', where the Mayor presided over cases involving claims of less than forty shillings. Beneath the Tholsel, in arched recesses many individuals sold fish.

In October 1812 the construction workers building a lighthouse on Tuskar Rock were overwhelmed by a storm and mountainous seas. Their shelters were washed away and survivors chained themselves to massive concrete blocks for four days awaiting rescue. The Wexford dead included Richard Meyler, John Edwards, William Bishop, William Devereux, Jasper Corish and J. Nowlan. The survivors were T. Barrington, Patrick Dillon and Nicholas Cahill.

In the same year a new gaol was built in Wexford at the corner of Hill Street and Spawell Road. It comprised of 58 cells and 16 airing yards and served for almost 100 years. The male prisoners spent their time on a treadmill or breaking stones, while the females were employed at washing, spinning and knitting. The walls of the gaol were 20 feet high and public executions were carried out on gallows erected on the gaol green up until the 1860s.

Fever Hospital was built in 1818 at the present Grogan's Road. It had 60 beds. Cholera epidemics were common in the busy seaport. The Presentation Nuns came to Wexford in that year. They opened their convent at Francis Street, then called James Street, on 2 October with the assistance of their benefactor, Mr. Carroll of The Faythe. There was a school for the girls of the town. The nuns undertook the education of the children of the Talbot Orphanage at Summerhill. The chapel of their convent was used for public Masses from 1826 to 1858. Saint Peter's College, which was opened in 1819, replacing a seminary at Michael Street established in 1811 by Bishop Ryan. St Peter's College trained priests for the diocese and abroad for almost 200 years.

Gentlemen's clubs were common and in 1828 the Brunswick Club was formed at the Assembly Rooms, the present day Arts Centre, in Cornmarket. The Brunswick was Protestant and Loyalist and preached against the nationalist cause. The Wexford Independent Club at the Commercial News Rooms was then established for those of a differing viewpoint.

Bishopswater Whiskey was produced in The Bishopswater Distillery, founded by Devereux and Harvey in 1827. The company had its own cooperage and cart-making shops and sold its product throughout the British Isles.

The Ballast Bank was built in 1831, to permit boats leaving port without cargo to take on ballast of rocks or sand for stability. Likewise, those arriving in ballast could deposit it and be ready for loading.

In 1832 the Wexford Dockyard was opened by John Redmond on reclaimed land to the south of the quays. The yard could build ships of up to 360 tons and the first boat completed there was 'The Vulcan', for Nathaniel Hughes, launched in 1833.

The Ballast Bank. (Rossiter Collection)

This picture is from an advertising booklet on Wexford Dockyard.

The year 1832 also saw a major cholera epidemic in Wexford. Two of the crew of the *Maria* died and rumours of epidemic spread through the town. There were ten doctors resident in Wexford at the time and all fought valiantly to contain the disease. The Fever Hospital was soon full. More accommodation was needed. A ship used to house prisoners during the 1798 Rebellion was commandeered and fitted as a hospital ship. It was moored in the Slaney, above the location of the present bridge and used to isolate the cholera victims. Still the epidemic raged. Between August and December 1832 over 130 people died of the disease and then the epidemic waned.

In January 1832, the Theatre Royal in High Street opened to the public. It was built for a Mr. Taylor, owner of the *Wexford Herald* newspaper and took the place of another playhouse, which had stood in Cornmarket, where Kelly's shop now trades. The magnificent Theatre Royal, lit by candles and oil lamps, attracted patrons from near and far. The vicinity of High Street was regularly filled with the carriages of the 'gentry' flocking to one of the finest theatres in any town of Wexford's size. It was common practice, after the show, to adjourn to Carr's Hotel in Oyster Lane for a supper of oysters, from Wexford Harbour, accompanied by brown bread and porter.

Wexford's first Catholic mayor was elected in 1833. He was William Whitty, a grain merchant from The Faythe.

In 1836 the Earl of Mulgrave, Viceroy of Ireland, arrived at the Courthouse on the quay accompanied by a company of Hussars. Cannon from a private collection of Grogan-Morgan of Johnstown Castle fired a salute on the quay. The Viceroy paraded along the waterfront, past the gas-works, up New Road (Parnell Street) to the Faythe and back along Main Street. After tea at Bettyville, near the present Wexford Racecourse, he attended a banquet at the Assembly Rooms, Cornmarket. The Earl left Wexford next morning.

Poet and composer Thomas Moore visited Wexford in 1835. Moore's mother was a daughter of Thomas Codd, who had lived in Cornmarket. The Thomas Moore Tavern is the house, and a plaque above the door commemorates the poet. Moore visited the Presentation Convent and planted a tree in the grounds after which he entertained the nuns with some of his music.

The firm of Pierce's was founded in 1839, making fire fans. It soon expanded to agricultural machinery and opened a factory at Mill Road. When a new bridge was being built at Carcur in 1856, the contract went to Pierce's. The enterprising company built their own machinery for completing the job. The bridge has since been demolished. Pierces went on to manufacture bicycles and munitions, but agriculture machinery was its forte and to service that market it had offices in Paris and Buenos Aires in the 1800s.

One year after a visit by Father Mathew on 10 April 1841, the Temperance Crusade began in Wexford with a rally attended by thousands in the grounds of the Franciscan Church. The Temperance Club was founded in a room at Clancy's, later The County Hotel, in Anne Street. At this first popular reading room in Wexford, for a subscription of one penny per week people had access to the newspapers of the day. It was popular due to a shortage of papers and as the news was read aloud, persons unable to read kept abreast of the things without embarrassment.

The Temperance Hall was built later adjoining the boundary wall of Selskar Abbey. The first secretary of the Temperance Club was Thomas D'Arcy Magee, politician, poet and author, who went on to become one of the founders of modern Canada. He was later assassinated in Ottawa.

On 8 December 1840 the Sisters of Mercy were established at a house on Paul Quay. At Summerhill they took over the Redmond Talbot Orphanage. Financially

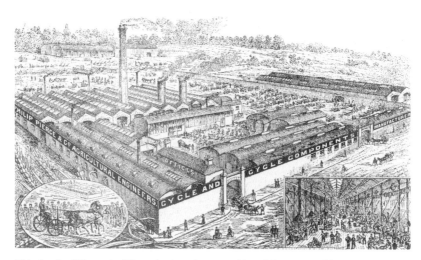

This sketch of Pierces in full production gives us an idea of the extent of the company in the late 1800s. It was published in 'The Event' in 1897.

This is Anne Street in the early 1900s.

(Lawrence Collection)

Here is another road that has altered completely. The Mercy Convent, orphanage and laundry stood here into the 1980s. (Rossiter Collection)

This is a copy of a page of the log of the ship 'Alert' referring to a voyage from Wexford to Odessa in the 1800s. (Private collection)

assisted by Richard Devereux they opened a convent and school at Summerhill. In 1856, they opened another school in George's Street and nine years later they established a House of Mercy at Summerhill to train girls as domestic servants. This enterprise was supported by a public laundry service, which lasted into the late 20th century.

Richard and John Thomas Devereux attended Mr. Behan's school in George Street. The Redmonds and James Roche, who would also to play a large part in the development of Wexford, were classmates. The brothers later attended the Protestant Diocesan School at Spawell Road. John Thomas and Richard formed a company called Devereux Brothers and were the principal shipowners in the town for over half a century. Richard Devereux owned forty boats that sailed under a flag with a letter D. He was a benefactor of most religious and educational groups coming to Wexford. He donated one hundred and twenty-three volumes of suitable material to every parish library in the area and set aside £30,000 for the relief of the poor. He was a Knight of Saint Gregory, a teetotaler and attended two Masses daily. He died in 1883 worth over a quarter of a million pounds in the currency of the time.

The Redmond family had started the Redmond Bank in Wexford in 1770 and was involved in business and shipping. Walter Redmond had two brothers, John and Patrick. Little is known of the latter but John had two sons, Patrick Walter and John Edward. In 1820 a bequest of Walter Redmond was used to establish the Redmond Talbot Orphanage at Summerhill. John Edward Redmond was a major force in land reclamation in Wexford Harbour, extension of the quays and the building of Wexford Dockyard.

Patrick Walter was the father of William Archer Redmond, M.P., and grandfather of John Edward Redmond MP, principal Lieutenant of Charles Stewart Parnell and a champion of Home Rule, who almost won Irish freedom by parliamentary means. Another grandson, William, was killed in action in the First World War in 1917. William is remembered in Wexford by Redmond Park on Spawell Road.

In 1840, the Irish Act abolished 38 Boroughs, including Wexford. The town lost its charter. Because the population exceeded 3,000 it could petition the Crown for a replacement. Wexford was the only town to pursue this and regained a Charter from Queen Victoria.

The Workhouse in Wexford accepted its first inmate in 1842. The Workhouse or Poor House, as it became known, was a common sight in an Ireland ravaged by famine in 1840s.

In the year 1837 there were 'six hundred and ninety Wexfordmen sailing in one hundred and ten registered vessels'. In addition, two ships sailed regular schedules between the town and Liverpool. Listed among the Wexford fleet of the time were: *The Forth* and *The Selskar* on the grain route to the Black Sea ports, The *Undine* which carried fruit from Patros (now Patra in Greece) and from Myrna (now Ismir in Turkey). *The Saltee* and *The Hantoon* sailed to Canada for timber; *The Wexford* carried emigrants from Liverpool to the southern states of America and returned with cotton. *The Menapia* sailed to West Africa, trading trinkets for palm oil. These were just some ships of a port which J. G. Kohl, a traveller in 1842, stated had 'more home-owned ships than any other in Ireland'.

Sir Francis Le Hunt erected a full-scale model of a sailing ship at a quarry near the Workhouse. On this deck and rigging, near Carcur, the boys of the Workhouse received training in seamanship and many are believed to have gone on to distinguished service at sea. One Wexford seaman who earned distinction was Henry Mullen of Abbey Street. While serving on the British ship *Trabolgan* he gave assistance to a Spanish ship found on fire in the Atlantic. In recognition of this act Queen Isabella of Spain had a special medal struck for the Wexfordman.

Twenty-seven schools served the population of the town in the 1800s according to the Dublin Almanac. Most of these would have been small classes held in private dwellings throughout the town. The principal school was the Diocesan at Spawell Road and the Infant School, which according to Kohl 'catered for ninety-one Catholic and thirty Protestant children' in 1842. All instruction was in verse and accompanied by actions. Examples given were 'This is the way we snuff the candle' or 'this is the way we churn the butter.'

The town received its final charter from Queen Victoria in 1846. It clearly defined the boundaries of the borough and established the wards of St Mary, St Selskar and St Iberius. Each ward was entitled to elect eight persons to the council but only residents having property of a value above £500 was permitted to stand for election.

Richard Devereux invited the newly formed Christian Brothers to Wexford to cater for the male population. Their school opened on 15 May 1849, on the site of today's John of God School in the Faythe. This catered mainly for boys from the south end of town. Within four years another school was started in George's Street. It was named the Dr. Sinnott School in memory of a Vicar of Ferns, who had advocated a school for boys of the north end. On the opening day 1 September 1853, its 192 places were filled immediately and over 80 boys had to be turned away. In 1874 Richard Devereux provided the Christian Brothers with a monastery at the Boker, where they still reside. Among the subjects taught in the boy's schools were navigation and astronomy.

The Mechanic's Institute at the top of Anne Street began operation on 13 July 1849.

It offered adult education classes (drawing was the first course offered), a museum and a library of books, periodicals and newspapers. The cost of membership was fixed as Apprentices 4/=, Operatives 6/= and others 10/= per annum. Life membership was available for five pounds cash or suitable books valued at ten pounds. Among, its rules were that no papers were to be read near the open fire and papers were not to be held for longer than fifteen minutes.

In 1851, work began on two new churches for Wexford. The foundation stones containing parchments detailing the names of the bishop, clergy, building fund committee, architect and contractor of both churches were blessed amid great ceremony on 27 June 1851. Funds for the twin churches were raised by many projects in the years shortly after the famine. Eminent members of the community contributed. Promises of donations were secured and the amounts collected in installments. Ships were visited and crewmen gave donations after each trip.

The churches were built within seven years at a cost of £26,6268 each. Mr. Willis, a local architect and builder, built them of Wicklow granite and sandstone from Park Quarry near Wexford. The railings were made and erected by Pierces and were painted and maintained free of charge for over a century by the company. The church at Bride Street is built on four acres near the site of an older church dedicated to Saint Bridget. Each church is one hundred and sixty-six feet long and 66 feet wide. The spires are two hundred and twenty-two feet from basement to pinnacle. The distance from main door to main door between both churches is five hundred and sixty yards.

Most people have to stop and think before getting the titles correct. They are better known by their location than the official titles. The Church of the Assumption is at Bride Street. The Church of the Immaculate Conception is at Rowe Street.

The Tate School, now Wexford's Municipal Buildings, was built in 1867, with money bequeathed by a Wexfordman named William Tate who made his fortune in Jamaica. The money was originally intended for his nephew George, but stories of his wild lifestyle caused a change in the will. The school was built for £1,632-6-1 and a further thousand pounds was invested, with the interest to be used to feed Wexford's poor. The Tate School operated as a boarding and day school into the 1940s.

Most Rev. Dr. Furlong, then Bishop of Ferns, founded the Sisters of St John of God in Wexford in 1871. The order began with seven sisters in a small house at Sallyville on Newtown Road. The larger convent was built in 1881 and still serves the order.

Another order of nuns appeared at Wexford in 1870. At the request of the bishop and with the assistance of Richard Devereux, Rockfield House, at Spawell Road, became the convent of the Sisters of Marie Reparatrix. In October 1874 a convent of Perpetual Adoration was established, which most of the original nuns entered. The twenty-four hour adoration of the Blessed Sacrament began on 1 January 1875, although Papal approval did not arrive until August of that year. The nuns only then adopted the distinctive red and white habit. The sisters moved to a convent adjoining the Church of the Assumption on 1 May 1887.

The railway then known as the Dublin-Wicklow-Wexford Railway (DWWR) reached Carcur (present day Boat Club) near Wexford on 17 August 1870. Four years later a station was opened at Slaney Street, today's North Railway Station. By 1882 trains were running to Rosslare. The line to Rosslare closed after 10 years but it was re-opened in 1894 to connect with a new mail boat service between Rosslare Harbour and Fishguard in south Wales. Special excursions were run on this line every Wednesday of the summer in 1896 and patrons were entertained on the pier at Rosslare Harbour by bands of the Wexford Militia and the Third Royal Irish Regiment. The original plan was for the railway line from Wexford to go on a landward route around the town. This proved too expensive and it eventually ran along the waterfront.

The first new cemetery in over one hundred years was opened on 1 May 1892 at Crosstown. The original plan had been to locate it at Mulgannon. This would be the first Wexford cemetery outside the growing town. A small graveyard principally for the Union Workhouse had opened earlier at Coolcotts but was not on consecrated ground. For centuries Wexford people had been interred in the graveyards of the old churches.

Opening a new cemetery was not an easy matter. There was a sworn enquiry about the overcrowding of the town graveyards with evidence given by Dr. John Creane and Dr. Thomas Pierse, both medical officers of health. The first person interred at Crosstown was a Quaker, Mrs. Johnson, the wife of Mordecai, from George's Street. She was buried on 16 October 1892. Her grave is at right angles to all other graves in Crosstown.

Land at Clonard purchased from St Peter's College in 1892 was enclosed and leveled. A handball alley seating four hundred was built. There was a cricket pitch, a football ground, a running track and a stand for six hundred spectators. Wexford Park

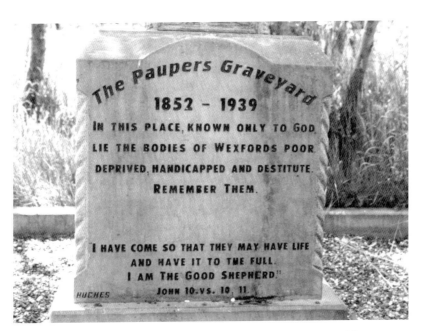

This stone is a recent addition to the graveyard in Coolcotts where inmates of the workhouse and the unidentified bodies from the harbour or of vagrants were buried between 1852 and 1939. (Rossiter Collection)

This picture dates from the 1950s when Cousins produced mineral waters at this factory in Peter's Square.

also had provision for show jumping and agricultural shows. In 1912 an air show was staged in the Park, and a plane actually took off from there, only to lose power and crash at the cott safe off Batt Street.

Race meetings were regularly held on the reclaimed lands at Ardcavan at the turn of the twentieth century. On 14 September 1900, many people from the town travelled over by boat, as was the custom. Road transport would have been via Carcur. Local trawlers supplemented their earnings by operating ferry services. One vessel the *Dolphin*, carried thirty-six passengers. Unable to dock at Ardcavan, the trawler had a small boat in tow for the transfer of passengers. At 3.30 pm fourteen people were landed from the *Dolphin*. The other twenty-two people crowded into the small boat to get ashore, causing it to lie low in the water. On the short trip to land water lapped into the craft. People panicked and the boat capsized. Despite the efforts of all who heard the cries for help seven people were drowned, Denis (29) and Catherine (28) Kenny, of High Street; William (20) and Martin (22) Blake of The Faythe-deep sea sailors; Mary Furlong (20) of William Street, who was about to be married; William Duggan (40) of Carrigeen who was the Bishop's coachman, and Patrick Doyle (22) of Distillery Road.

When cars began to be registered in Wexford the numbers were preceded by the letter MI and the registration MI 1 went to Colonel J.R. Magrath of Bann-a Boo, Wexford. The first nine cars owners had rural addresses and it was at MI 10 we find V.G. Piggott of Glena Terrace with a town address.

In 1906 Wexford's Foundries employed 600, the Hat Factory had 100, the Distillery 50, Cousins Mineral Water 50, Thompson's, constructing hay sheds employed 50 and the Dockyard had 60 employees.

We apologise for the quality on this picture of 'scab' workers escorted by the Royal Irish Constabulary during the Lockout of 1911.

THE LOCKOUT OF 1911

The population of Wexford in 1911 was eleven thousand, five hundred and thirty-one. A large number depended on the foundries for their livelihood. Of the foundries, Pierces was the largest employing four hundred men mainly in the manufacture of agricultural machinery and bicycles. The other foundries were Wexford Engineering, known as the 'Star', in Trinity Street opened in 1882 and Doyle's, Selskar Iron Works, at Redmond Road opened in 1897.

Trade unions were beginning to emerge as a potent force. A dock strike, affecting the whole of the British Isles, was underway and the dockers of Wexford Port joined it on 8 July 1911. Their demand for a wage increase, a ten-hour working day and the abolition of night work was conceded on 21 July. Wexford workers now recognised the power of organisation.

The Irish Transport and General Workers Union spread from the docks to the foundries. By 16 August large numbers of foundry men had joined. History began to repeat itself. After a dock strike in 1890, members of Pierces staff had become unionized, but all trade unionists had been dismissed. The management in 1911 attempted the same tactics. Pierce warned that the company would close if the men persisted in joining the union. This time the workers held firm. On 26 August all 400 men were locked out.

On 31 August William Hearne, whose family owned Wexford Engineering, told his employees that only those who rejected the union need report for work after the weekend. On Monday morning only one man was at the gate. Doyle Brothers closed their premises without giving any reason. The employers had accepted the unions for apprenticed tradesmen for some years. They were fearful of unskilled or semi-skilled employees joining the militant Irish Transport Union founded by Jim Larkin in 1909.

With all the foundries in Wexford closed or under threat of closure, Peter T. Daly, southern organiser of the union addressed a large crowd at the Bullring. He pointed out that the men denied the right to work had made no demand other than the freedom to belong to a trade union.

At Pierces, fourteen policemen escorted eight foremen attempting to keep the business going to and from work. Pickets at the gates often numbered five hundred and this led to one hundred and fifty police reinforcements being brought to Wexford. Conciliation talks suggested that the men be allowed join a union for their specific skill or that a solely Wexford union be formed.

James Larkin, a leader of the ITGWU., arrived in town and addressed a large crowd at the Faythe. He derided the employers for the hypocrisy of their offer. He pointed out that men without recognised skills could not join a craft union. As for a local union, he asked if employers would accept a local market only. The gates remained locked.

Unrest grew. Police baton-charged picketers and in one incident Michael O'Leary received fatal injuries. O'Leary's funeral was one of the largest seen on Wexford's streets.

Families of those locked out were reduced to existing on one meal per day. Most depended on friends and relatives for food. Money for the families was raised at church gates. The Gaelic Athletic Association organised benefit matches. The proceeds of the Leinster Final between Dublin and Kilkenny were used to support the strikers. There was great support also from middle class individuals, the Ancient Order of Hibernians and from rural workers. To their credit Wexford Corporation did not press those locked out for arrears of rent.

In October, the foundries announced that they would re-open with non-union labour. Within days, they claimed that more workers than they could hire had abandoned the union. These men were employed at Pierces and Selskar Iron Works. In Pierces Mill Road Works beds and cookers were installed so that those at work could avoid contact with the picketers.

Mr. Peter Daly addressing a rally in the Faythe, only a few hundred yards from Pierces, drew enormous response with the cry:

'We beat "No papist need apply"; we beat "No Irish need apply" and we will beat "No transport union need apply".'

The dockers, in support of those locked out blockaded delivery of coke to the factories. Therefore manufacturing was impossible and the 'black legs' could only be engaged in assembly, painting and dispatch of stock on hand from before the lockout. Pickets, booing and stone throwing, with police constantly intervening accompanied all the shipments of that stock to the quayside. The 'black leg' workers were also harassed as they were escorted for recreation to farms outside Wexford town. Seventeen weeks after the first lockout newspapers and clergy urged the men to abandon the fight. Christmas was approaching with little prospect of good cheer. The workers remained loyal to their cause.

During January 1912, James Connolly arrived in Wexford at James Larkin's request. With Peter Daly's arrest some days later for inciting people to violence, he took charge of negotiations. By early February, an agreement was reached. The foundries agreed to recognise an Irish Foundry Workers Union. They were free to employ non-union members, within limits. There would be no victimisation. All reinstatements would be carried out through the new union. At a victory rally in the Faythe on 9 February Connolly said that the result could be called a draw, but that the workers had won their fight.

The lockout brought onto the political scene Richard Corish, then a pattern maker in Wexford Engineering. Corish became a member of the Lockout Committee and was arrested on numerous occasions for harassing 'black legs'. He went on to become Mayor of Wexford in 1920, a position he held for a record twenty-five consecutive years until his death in 1945. He also represented Wexford in Dail Eireann where he was succeeded by his son Brendan, who became Leader of the Labour Party and Deputy Prime Minister (Tanaiste).

CHAPTER FOUR

THE FIRST WORLD WAR,
THE CIVIL WAR AND
THE SECOND WORLD WAR

WORK BEGAN IN APRIL OF 1914 to transform a warehouse where salvaged goods were often sold into the Palace Cinema at Harpur's Lane – note the correct name. This was Wexford's first purpose built cinema. Films had been shown at the Theatre Royal previously and in other venues as were common in the era. It was to seat 600 and the cinema and the lane outside would be lighted by electricity.

The first Wexford corps of Volunteers was formed in 1914. This national force had been growing rapidly for months, rallying to 'The Cause of Irish Independence'. The Wexford corps grew from a meeting at the Assembly Rooms in Cornmarket at which Liam Mellowe's announced that Mr. Stafford had offered the use of his premises at Gibson's Lane (Peter's Street) for drilling of recruits. Within weeks there were 200 Volunteers drilling three times per week and exchanging military salutes in the street.

When the third reading of the Home Rule Bill at Westminster was passed a massive parade and demonstration took place in Wexford. At the request of the Mayor all businesses closed at 8 pm on Wednesday 27 May to facilitate those taking part. Bunting and national flags flew from all buildings and from ships in the harbour. The monuments in the Bullring and Redmond Place were lighted and rockets and fireworks filled the air. Rockets were fired from the Fort at Rosslare in reply.

With trouble in Dublin later in the year when the Scottish Border Regiment Members fired on civilians there was a huge increase in Volunteer numbers in Wexford. Over 200 workers from Pierces Foundry marched en masse from St Peter's Square to Wexford Park to enlist. The Volunteer strength soon exceeded 700.

On 1 August 1914, the local newspaper The Free Press carried a small story under the heading 'WAR-AUSTRIA v. SERVIA'. By 8 August the headline read 'EUROPE IN FLAMES'. The Great War had begun. Soon there came day-by-day accounts of the war and the atrocities, with appeals for men to join the army.

Life went on. Wexford played Kerry in an All-Ireland Football Final and lost.

HORSES FOR THE ARMY

OWNERS OF HORSES SUITABLE AS

CHARGERS, CAVALRY RIDERS AND ARTILLERY DRAUGHT FOR ARMY PURPOSES,

And who are desirous of selling to the Government buyers are requested not to clip their Horses.

It is necessary that Horses intended for Active Service during the Winter months shall be unclipped.

The co-operation of all owners is invited to carry out this most essential detail.

An advertisement from 1914.

The shop workers week was reduced to five and a half days, with the introduction of half-day closing on Thursdays. Mayor Sinnott and Lady Maurice Fitzgerald of Johnstown Castle officially opened the Palace Cinema on 7 December. The proceeds from the first event, a concert, went to the welfare of Belgian refugees of the war settled at Gorey. The first film shown in the Palace was *The Old Maid's Baby*, starring John Bunny, and it was accompanied by film of the Wexford-Kerry All-Ireland Final. Filmed local events were the most popular feature of the early cinema.

In 1915 the local press referred constantly to Wexfordmen being involved in various battles. They were among the wounded at Gallipoli. Wexford sailors were the heroes of many shipping attacks and calls continued for recruits. In June a major recruiting rally was held at the Bullring. The band of the Royal Dublin Fusiliers attended *and Magic Lantern* slides of atrocities in Belgium were projected on to the side of a van. Rumours spread through the town that the Distillery was to be used as a prisoner of war camp – these proved false. The local force of the Volunteers was given use of the Military Barracks and Wexford was well represented at a rally of 30,000 reviewed by John Redmond MP. in the Phoenix Park, Dublin.

On 13 November it was announced that munitions would be manufactured at Pierce's. With falling orders for agricultural machinery in Europe due to the war this new enterprise gave jobs to many who would otherwise have been unemployed. Men and women worked in shifts at the foundry making shell casings.

In April 1916 came news of the Easter Rising in Dublin. Rebel nationalists took Enniscorthy. Steps were taken for the defence of Wexford. The Volunteers were placed at the disposal of the Royal Irish Constabulary and 500 Wexford citizens, including the Mayor, were enlisted as special constables. The town was on the alert. Within days 150 troops arrived from Fermoy to assist the RIC. Later extra military in the form of infantry, artillery and cavalry were camped at Drinagh, south of the town.

The homes of Sinn Fein supporters and other 'suspects' were raided on Saturday 6 May. Among those arrested was Richard Corish. St Brigid's Home for Inebriates (formerly the gaol and now The County Hall) the Royal Irish Constabulary Barracks at 69 South Main Street (now Dun Mhuire) and the Military Barracks at Barrack Street were used as prisons until the detainees could be sent to Dublin. Most were released within a month. The extra troops departed from Wexford within two weeks and the Mayor congratulated the citizens of the town for their calm and quiet conduct throughout. The Rising was over but the Great War continued and Wexford men still died in foreign fields.

At home the increasing costs of ingredients caused Wexford bakers to announce an end to the practice of giving away free barm bracks at Christmas.

In 1918, the United States Air Force operated a Sea Plane Base across the Slaney, at Ferrybank. For the last months of the war the sight of planes taking off and landing on the river was commonplace for the people of Wexford.

John Redmond died in London in 1918 and his body was returned to Wexford for burial. In one of the largest funerals for years in the town he was laid to rest in the family vault at St John's Cemetery.

On 21 April 1918, the Old Pound, St Peter's Square, was the scene of an anti-conscription protest. Rev. Mark O'Byrne, Fr. Ryan, Richard Corish, James Sinnott and J. J. Stafford addressed a crowd of over 5,000.

Influenza, the epidemic that followed the Great War, reached Wexford in 1918. Schools closed and elaborate precautions were taken at factories. The Infirmary and Workhouse were filled with over 1,000 people afflicted. At this time the Palace Cinema included in it's advertising the slogan 'Cinema disinfected daily with Jeyes Fluid'.

Wexford was in darkness in 1918 caused by a strike at the Gasworks. This was before a national electricity grid existed and gas fired street lighting was in use. In addition there was no automation, a person went around at dusk lighting lamp standards

This is a photo from 1918 of the United States Air Force base across the river Slaney at Ferrybank. (Wally Doyle collection)

The Redmond family vault at
John's Street graveyard.
(Rossiter Collection)

individually and extinguished them at dawn. Luckily the strike was short, as it had also closed most of the factories.

As the war ended Irish politics came to the fore. Fr. O'Flanagan, vice-president of Sinn Fein, addressed a meeting at Peter's Square, in support of local Dail candidate Mr. Jim Ryan. When fighting erupted between rival groups the RIC. baton charged the crowd. At the end of the meeting the square was cordoned off by police and the Sinn Fein supporters were only allowed to leave via Peter's Street, with an escort. In the election on Saturday, 14 December 1918, Sinn Fein won the seats for County Wexford North and South.

Countess Markievicz visited Wexford early in 1919. A crowd of over 2,000 met her at Carcur and they paraded through Wexford to the Talbot Hotel. Many tricolours were in evidence.

In April 1920, a national strike was called to support the political prisoners on hunger strike in Mountjoy Prison. At noon on Tuesday, 13 April at the request of the Labour Party, all work stopped in Wexford, with the exception of bakeries and provision stores. Passengers arriving on the mail boat at Rosslare Harbour had to walk to their destination. A parade of support was held in Wexford in which the Volunteers and Cumann Na mBan participated. On Wednesday morning pickets were placed on banks and other premises that had remained open. By noon the prisoners were released and Wexford returned to business as usual on Thursday morning.

As a result of continuing raids on private houses, all civilian guns were to be voluntarily surrendered to the military and a large number were collected. In June

400 extra troops arrived via Rosslare Harbour. Their destination was Wexford Military Barracks.

Forty members of the Devonshire Regiment, stationed at the Barracks, ran amok on Wexford's streets in September. They accosted civilians with demands to know where the Sinn Fein Club was and they assaulted people. The RIC tried to intervene but their requests for assistance to troops at the Barracks were ignored. The local people could take no more and hit back. Fights broke out on the Main Street and at the Bullring, stones and bottles were thrown. Eventually the soldiers were driven back to the headquarters.

By October 1920, there were widespread military raids on homes and businesses. People were stopped on the streets and ordered to line up along the wall at gunpoint. The names and occupations of the men were taken and their pockets searched.

On 15 January 1921, Martial Law was declared.

Among the regulations were:

'No dances to be organised without permission of the military commander.

No collections to be taken up without express permission.

Fairs and marts were suspended.

Possession of arms was punishable by death.

Unauthorized wearing of British military uniform was punishable by death.

Name, age, sex and occupation of every person resident in a house or flat had to be displayed inside the main door.

Loitering was forbidden.

Meetings were banned; any group of six or more was classed as a meeting.

The use of carrier pigeons was prohibited and all pigeon lofts were to open to inspection.'

Apologies for the quality but this rare photograph is from an old newspaper. It shows Michael Collins posing with a Pierce bicycle on a visit to the foundry in 1922.

By February the infamous 'Black and Tans' had arrived in Ireland. These were an irregular military force, recruited to supplement the RIC. It is commonly believed that their ranks included many criminals and other misfits. Their time in Ireland was one of great unrest and constant atrocities and reprisals. Many Wexford people still recall the harassment and prohibitions of those days. Masked men looking for official letters to the RIC or the military raided the General Post Office. In June the District Inspector of the Royal Irish Constabulary was wounded in the leg by shots fired near his home in the Distillery Lane area. A major search during which all public houses were ordered to close at 9pm, failed to find the assailants.

The Free Press headline of 10 December 1921, read- 'We Have Won Our Liberty'

The treaty had been signed. On Sunday, 9 April 1922, Michael Collins spoke to a record crowd in Peter's Square, who applauded the treaty. Collins was presented with a set of pipes. He attended 11 am Mass at the Friary and later visited Pierces where he is said to have expressed a wish that the company supply its famous bicycles for the National Army.

The uneasy peace was short-lived. A headline of 8 July 1922, proclaimed – 'Tragedy Of A Nation'. The Civil War had begun. Wexford's Executive Military who were anti-treaty took up position in the streets and strategic approaches to the town. They took over Rowe's Mill at Spawell Road (now part of Redmond Park), Nolan's of Redmond Place, opposite Redmond Monument, the Custom Offices on the Quay and Walshe's of Glena Terrace, at the bottom of Hill Street. The Mechanic's Institute at Main Street was commandeered as a First Aid Station. A curfew of 11 pm was imposed, but largely ignored by the townspeople who strolled the streets discussing the situation. The first Wexford casualty of the Civil War was a man from Belmullet who worked in the town. He was killed by a shotgun blast at Monck Street.

Another historic advertisement announces the planned meeting to be addressed by Michael Collins in 1922. Note the lower advertisement curtailing the sale of drink on the day.

The National Army reached Wexford in the afternoon of Sunday 9 July The force of 200 men with armoured cars entered the town and arrested people at Oliver Plunkett Street and at the RIC barracks. The National Army had control by 22 July.

In October 1922, four local members of the National Army were killed by a bomb dropped on their car from the Railway Bridge at Ferrycarrig. The dead soldiers were from Coolcotts, Talbot Street, Hill Street and Broadway, a village about 10 miles south of town.

At 8 pm on 13 March 1923, three men, James Parle, John Creane and Patrick Hogan were executed by firing squad at the Gaol in Hill Street, behind the County Hall. The three young men had been caught in possession of firearms, some days earlier. The number of Wexford people who died in the wars between 1914 and 1923 has never been calculated.

THE THIRTIES:

In 1932 The Eucharistic Congress was held in Dublin. Church dignitaries from around Europe travelled through Wexford having arrived in the country by sea via Rosslare Harbour. Cardinal Roey of Belgium stopped in the town where much fundraising and support had been organised for his countrymen during the Great War. The first cardinal in modern times to visit Wexford went in procession from the North Railway Station to the Church of the Assumption where prayers were offered. For the early morning visit large crowds, many from rural areas, thronged the streets.

Industry was thriving in the 1930s, Wexford Paint and Varnish Company at King Street manufactured Capitol Paint in a factory located behind the Capitol Cinema, Slaney Minerals had a bottling plant in Batt Street and Brockhouse manufactured springs and became known locally as 'Springs', had their factory located at Maudlintown.

Drama, concerts, lectures and rallies were popular at the Theatre Royal and in the cinemas. Dancing was another activity of the period and a very popular venue was the Whiterock Social Club. The club situated on a hill near Bishopswater was accessible only along unevenly paved and unlighted roads but attracted crowds from the town and outlying areas. The Whiterock Club like many others had its own mummers who entertained neighbours in their houses.

ANOTHER WAR:

In September 1939, *The Free Press* reported the German invasion of Poland. The first effects were economic. The price of coal increased almost immediately. There was panic buying of sugar and petrol, leading to shortages.

The 'Blackout' entailed the town being kept invisible to aircraft at night. Exposed lights were forbidden. Streetlights remained off and all windows had to be completely covered. The reasons for the blackout were twofold, sighting of Wexford by German planes could help them plot the positions of a British town or a lighted Wexford could be mistaken for a British town and attacked. On the first weekend of October 1939 people congregated on the dark streets nightly discussing the situation. Booklets on air raids and other war-related precautions were distributed. Within days refugees were arriving from mainland Britain. These were mostly families of Irishmen working there.

Gasmasks and ration books were soon part of everyday Wexford life.

A major advertising campaign began, to recruit men for the Irish Army. In tandem with that a local force was formed to protect the country from invasion. The local force

Eamon DeValera is seen inspecting the LDF (Local Defence Force) at The Faythe in 1941.
(Rossiter Collection)

had a number of separate divisions. There was a coastal watch service, whose lookout posts dotted the shoreline. The Corporation recruited Air Raid Wardens, Auxiliary Firemen, First Aid Workers, Demolition and Rescue Workers and Decontamination Workers. A great fear at the time was that gas attacks would be unleashed. The LDF (or Local Defence Force), forerunners of the FCA were parading 300 men by July 1940. The members of the force, volunteers from all walks of life, drilled two nights per week at various sites around the town. Local men who had served in the British Forces instilled much of the military discipline. Drilling was done with a variety of weapons, from rifles to shotguns to dummy wooden guns. The more lethal weapons were kept under guard at the barracks. Manouvres were called at any hour of the day or night and many a cold dawn saw these deadly serious soldiers on the coast near Rosslare. The LDF was a prime force and the pride of Wexford as they paraded accompanied by private cars and commercial vans, volunteered by their owners for use in an emergency.

German aircraft attacked the *St Patrick* en-route from Rosslare Harbour to Fishguard on 18 August 1940. Moses Brennan from Ram Street, Wexford, a crewmember, was killed by machinegun fire.

In 1941 the Corporation advertised for tenders for the construction of air raid shelters. Each was to accommodate fifty people and to be located as follows: One at Cornmarket; two at the Town Hall, also in Cornmarket; two at the New Market in

These pictures from an old newspaper show the funeral of Captain Dick O'Neill of The Kerlogue in Lisbon.

the Bullring; one at Selskar; one at St Patrick's Square; four at St Peter's Square; two at King Street; one at the Crescent.

Although the town was never bombed it did witness a number of aerial dogfights between British and German planes. One such fight occurred circling the spires of the twin churches as people made their way to the Men's Confraternity. The planes eventually broke off and flew cover the coast. Such encounters often produced fatal results and a number of German airmen were buried at Crosstown cemetery after being shot down.

On Friday, 13th June 1941, 'The St Patrick' sailing from Rosslare Harbour was sunk 18 miles from the Welsh coast. Seventeen officers and crew and twelve passengers died in the nighttime machine gun and bomb attack. Among the dead was Michael Brennan of Ram Street, Wexford. His father had been killed during a previous attack on the same ship.

Throughout the war Wexford merchant ships continued to operate. The *Menapia*, sailed to the United States protected only by a tricolour painted on her superstructure. Other local ships involved in carrying supplies through hostile waters were: *Begerin*, *Edenvale* and *Gold Finder*. Another Wexford ship, *Kerlogue*, sailing from Lisbon picked up 167 German seamen from a sinking ship. In spite of British warnings, and against the required procedure of calling to a British port first, she landed her human cargo at Cobh.

In World War Two, the vessels *Irish Pine* and *The Cymric* were sunk and among the dead were at least four Wexfordmen.

CHAPTER FIVE

INTO THE MODERN ERA

THE INAUGURATION OF THE IRISH Republic was marked in Wexford in 1949 with a huge procession through the town. The FCA, the Old IRA, members of political parties and social clubs, marched with other uniformed bodies and the town's bands from the Military Barracks via Main Street, Rowe Street and School Street to St Peter's Square. There the tricolour flew at half-mast. Brendan Corish TD., read the 1916 Proclamation and the flag was raised. Three volleys were fired by the F.C.A. The bands played *Faith of Our Fathers* and the National Anthem, and then led the parade back to Barrack Street.

Wexford and Ireland of the 1950s had strong and freely expressed religious feelings. On Wednesday 1 November 1950, the Roman Catholic Church declared as dogma the Assumption of Our Blessed Lady into Heaven. Because one of our twin churches is dedicated to the Assumption, celebrations in the town were on a grand scale. The whole of Wexford was decorated with flags and lights. Altars were displayed in the windows of shops and private houses. Church services were thronged. The overflowing crowds filled the churchyards. Bonfires blazed in the streets and the town's bands paraded to the churches, both morning and evening.

Mass X-Ray vans arrived in Wexford for the first time in September 1951. The mobile units were the frontline troops in a battle to eradicate tuberculosis in Ireland. The killer disease, also called consumption, was widespread and claimed the lives of many including young adults. The x-ray units visited the factories, schools and shopping areas, where people stepped in, removed jewellery and medals, took a deep breath, were photographed and returned to their business. Those infected with the disease were detected on the x-rays, diagnosed and treated. Within a few years the scourge of TB was under control.

The beginning of a major cultural event in Wexford, the Wexford Opera Festival took place in 1951. The brainchild of Dr Tom Walsh, Dr. Des Ffrench, Eugene

The statue of John Barry, founder of the American Navy, is situated at The Crescent. (Rossiter collection)

McCarthy, a hotelier and Seamus Dwyer, a postman, took shape at the Theatre Royal. The first production was *Rose of Castile* by Balfe, who by coincidence had lived for a time in Wexford on North Main Street. Lord Longford, whose touring theatre group had often played at the Theatre Royal, opened the first festival. The opera festival was to grow into a top class international event, with many fringe events embracing all forms of art. The policy of staging top quality but often neglected operas proved a winner. One of the benefits of this festival has been the blossoming of latent artistic talents in Wexford people.

The American people presented a statue of John Barry, father of the United States Navy, to Wexford. The presentation had been agreed in the 1930s but the outbreak of war delayed implementation. The statue eventually arrived via Rosslare Harbour on board a United States Navy vessel. President Sean T. O'Kelly performed the unveiling ceremony on 16 September 1956, at the Crescent.

Polio came under concerted attack in the latter years of the decade. People can recall the visits to the County Clinic at Grogan's Road for the sugar lump, which was used to administer the oral vaccine – a major step forward from the anti-vaccination protest of the earlier part of the century.

In 1959 a new bridge opened connecting the town to Ferrybank. It is almost but not exactly on the site of the oak bridge of the 1790s where many of the victims of the insurrection died.

Dun Mhuire, the Parish Hall, was opened on 4 December 1960, with a concert by the Artane Boys' Band. Tickets cost from 2/6 to ten shillings. The first dance in the hall was to the music of Maurice Mulcahy and his fifteen-piece orchestra on December 13th. Admission to the dance cost 6/-.

The major event in Wexford for 1963 was the visit of John Fitzgerald Kennedy to the town on 27 June. The descendant of a County Wexford emigrant arrived by helicopter at Wexford Park on that Thursday morning. His motorcade, a sight never before seen in Wexford, passed through Summerhill, Grogan's Road, Roche's Road, Bride Street, Stonebridge, Lower King Street and Paul Quay proceeding to a wreath laying ceremony at the Barry Memorial on the Crescent. They then proceeded to Redmond Place where the President received the Freedom of Wexford from Mayor Thomas F. Byrne. The motorcade returned to the Park via Redmond Road and Carcur. Along the route the President stopped to greet nuns who stood outside the County Hospital, Loreto Convent and John of God Convent. The presidential visit was tinged with sadness by the illness of Dr. Staunton, Bishop of Ferns, who died shortly afterwards and whose funeral was attended by thousands of dignitaries and clergy and lay people. The assassination of President Kennedy in November of the same year brought great sadness to the town.

The Star Engineering Works, one of the Lockout Foundries, became an assembly plant for Renault cars and the first Wexford assembled Renault 8 drove through the factory gates on Tuesday 23 November 1965.

The big mystery of 1965 was, who had climbed the steeple jacks ladders on the night 18 and 19 July and placed a balaclava on the spire of the Church of the Assumption, Bride Street. The sight and the speculation kept people amused for days.

This photo is from an old newspaper cutting. It shows the funeral cortege of the airhostess on the St. Phelim that crashed off Tuskar Rock. It is turning on to Wexford Bridge.

Sunday 24 March 1968, was a traumatic day in Wexford. On that bright spring morning an Aer Lingus Viscount aircraft *St Phelim*, crashed without survivors off the Wexford coast. The weeks that followed were filled with tales of the search for bodies and wreckage. Poignant scenes accompanied the funerals as they passed through the town. Sixty one people died in the tragedy, one an air hostess whose family was from Wexford.

LATTER DAYS

In dealing with the Wexford of the last few decades, one loses much of the necessary perspective, which enables a proper unbiased picture of a vibrant town. Judgment is clouded by personal involvement in some of the events that occurred. Therefore we paint the canvas of these decades in very broad strokes.

Decimalization was introduced, as was one-way traffic on the Main Street.

This recalls the twinning ceremony with Coueron in 1982 at the old town wall in Abbey Street. Matt Stafford (town sergeant) holds the ceremonial mace, Jimmy Mahoney, former Wexford stevedore and corporation member is next and then almost hidden is Mayor Padge Reck and the Mayor of Coueron. (Rossiter Collection)

Good bye £.s.d

SHILLINGS AND PENCE, happy companions with CORRY'S and their customers for years and years and years. To mark the occasion on FRIDAY AND SATURDAY, 12th and 13th FEBRUARY, 1971, our customers are offered SPECIAL BARGAINS. When did your purchase the following goods with the prices as normal ?

STOCKINGS (NYLON)	9d. pair
PINARETTES	2/11 each
DUTCH APRONS	2/11 each
HANDWOVEN TWEED 30″	6/11 yd.
LADIES' SUITS	£2-9-11 each
LADIES' DRESSES	10/11 and 19/11 each

Corry & Co.

13 & 15 North Main St., Wexford

A "DECIMAL SHOP" on 15th February, 1971.

This advertisement from the final issue of The Free Press reminds us of the change over to decimal currency in 1971.

The decades in question were ones of major expansion, particularly on the housing front. New houses were built in both Local Authority and private schemes. The population balance shifted to the western suburbs. So great was this increase that a new church was built in Clonard in 1974 in order to serve the needs of the relatively young population settling there. In 1975 a new parish of Clonard was created, totally separate from the town parishes.

On New Year's Eve 1975, Wexford was struck by a major rail disaster. The morning train to Dublin was derailed near Gorey and five people were killed. Throughout the day, reports and rumours of casualties were rife in the town. Of the dead, two were natives of the town.

On purpose built industrial estates on our outskirts factories with their head offices in Germany, America and Australia, began manufacturing. These firms supplemented and sadly in some instances replaced many local and traditional companies. The foundries are gone. In 1982 Wexford was twinned with the French town of Coueron in an open-air ceremony beside the old town wall in Abbey Street. This is interesting in that a new alliance between Wexford and France took place beside a wall built after invaders who came originally from France took the town.

In the past two decades Wexford has become acutely aware of its historic roots. The development of the international port at Rosslare Harbour has brought about a major influx of tourists to the region and to its principal town. To complement this development, the Irish National Heritage Park was established on the outskirts of Wexford at Ferrycarrig. There in a unique location the story of the region from pre-history to Norman times has been re-created. To complement this an interpretative centre was opened at Westgate in a building adjoining the last remaining gates of the old Norman town. There an audiovisual presentation can transport you back through the history and development of Wexford. The residents and visitors may still enjoy and marvel at the work of those who preceded us on the streets of Carman, Menapia, Weisfiord or Wexford.

THE MISCELLANY

E VERY TOWN AND VILLAGE HAS its history. This chronology of events determines the heritage, the origins and the character of the place and the people. But a timeline history cannot tell the full story, unless it took up numerous volumes and was littered with footnotes and references. To add that extra seasoning to our look at Wexford I am including this miscellany section. In essence, it contains the facts, figures and anecdotes that cannot easily fit into either the history or our guided tour. This section can be delved into at random and we hope that it will illuminate the story of Wexford and maybe mystify and amaze you at times.

THE HARBOUR COMMISSIONERS

In years past, Wexford Harbour Commissioners were a major force in a town dominated by a thriving port. Even with usage and revenue in decline, the meetings of this important body were reported weekly in the newspapers, as avidly as those of the Corporation or County Council. To give a flavour of the type of concerns that exercised the minds of the Harbour Commissioners, we provide some excerpts from their minutes and reports.

THE GREAT WAR

4 August 1914 – Night sailings of all vessels have been suspended and wireless apparatuses have been removed from ships in the area. Tuskar lighthouse and the lightships beams have been extinguished until further notice. A half company of the Shropshire Regiment is at Ballygeary sinking entrenchments and erecting a masked fort and field gun on the cliffs.

12 September 1914 – Work on the discharge of cargoes at Wexford Quays is being delayed because the majority of porters and labourers are being mobilised as members of the naval and army reserve.

20 September 1914 – British ship, *City of Hamburg* is being held in Germany, among the crew are Wm. Molloy, Peter Murphy of Parnell St and John Quirke of Waterloo Road.

21 October 1914 – About 250 men of the Wexford Battalion marched to Clonard and engaged in manouvres.

LIGHTING

In March 1916 Wexford Gas Company wrote to say that over £ 71 was owed and that lights on the quays would be put out if payment was not made before 1 April.

In September 1928 the Electricity Supply Board sent plans for the lighting of the quays and side streets to the board and asked for a decision before 'the coming winter'

In October 1928 there was a discussion on whether to use steel or wooden poles. No definite decision was made as the steel was more costly than wood.

In July 1930 there was a letter from the ESB. It proposed to supply lamps and fittings on any of the existing standards in the harbour free of charge. It was suggested that for sufficient lighting, 26 lamps should be erected.

NOVEMBER 1917

There was a letter from the Town Clerk with a report from the Medical Officer of Health relating to sanitary condition of lane adjacent to Charlotte Street. A committee was appointed to inspect the lane.

AUGUST 1925

The estimated cost of re-surfacing Anne Street was £ 10-8-0.

In December of the same year there was a letter from N. Lambert and J. Sinnott requesting permission to open Anne Street in order to lay water pipes and extend the entrance to Lambert's Bakery. Permission was granted provided the road was restored to its previous condition afterwards.

CAREER AT SEA IN 1944

Captain Freyne gave a lecture on *The Sea as a Career* at the Technical School.

Parents or guardians of intending sailors were urged to ensure that the boys did not suffer from flat feet, varicose veins or hernias and that their eyesight was good. He did not recommend the career as a means of curing tuberculosis. He said that a good practice was to send the boys away on a cadet ship. This cost about £ 100 a year and those unable to afford it should try to get an apprenticeship through the Technical School.

CRESCENT

In May 1945 discussions took place about the filling of the Crescent and the acquisition of the Ballast Bank. The chairman said that a person was interested in it but he could not divulge his name.

In August 1945 the County Manager proposed to fill in the Crescent to straighten the road and provide a small public garden and parking space. Alderman Moran suggested using it as a bus stop and to store pit wood and other items awaiting shipment. Mr. Saville had no objections to trees being planted there. Mayor James Sinnott said that it had been his desire the past number of years to see the Crescent used as a swimming pool and had advocated this to the corporation on numerous occasions.

THE OTHER FESTIVAL

Wexford Festival Opera is well established and world-renowned but there was another Wexford Festival back in the 1970s. Wexford Festival of Living Music was an ambitious undertaking but even the title got some backs up as they saw it as a slight on opera, inferring that it wasn't living music.

In March 1971 Tapestry Theatre a group of young people aiming to put Wexford on the arts map staged the first Wexford Festival of Living Music.

On that St Patrick's week their first series of events kicked off with booking reported as coming in from Britain, Holland and the United States and hotels and guesthouses appearing delighted with the prospects.

The Theatre Royal was the venue for two concerts. The first featured Danny Doyle, The Johnstons and The Strawbs. Another had The Chieftains as one of the acts. In The Abbey Cinema there was live music from Southern Comfort and Curved Air on one night and Dr. Strangely Strange and Fairport Convention on a later date. Meanwhile in Dun Mhuire Mellow Candle, Tir na nOg and Principal Edwards Magic Theatre filled the bill.

In addition, the festival featured a John McCormack record recital and museum at Whites Hotel. Murder in The Cathedral was staged in St Iberius Church and poets like Peter Fallon and Brendan Kennelly gave readings. The Ulster Youth Orchestra performed and Monica Carr provided a lecture and 'cook-in' at the Talbot Hotel.

The following year, despite financial problems Tapestry Theatre were again attracting top acts of the day to Wexford. In The Abbey The Chieftains and Shades of McMurrough provided the entertainment. At Dun Mhuire Horslips and Supply Demand and Curve were the featured artistes. The final concert had Planxty and East of Eden in The Abbey where there were reports of revelers dancing on the balcony wall. Each concert cost 50p admission. In addition late night film shows for 20p each featured Easy Rider, Yellow Submarine and Let It Be.

Local headlines a week later:

'Living Music Festival Slammed'

'It Mustn't Happen Again'

'Wexford Recovers from Hippy Invasion'

There was public outrage and indignation. Reports of young people sleeping together in doorways, the old sawmill at The Crescent being dubbed a 'Hippy Hostel' and some window breaking by an unruly element saw recriminations and counter claims as to the reasons in local newspapers but in the end, Living Music was killed in it's infancy.

LOOKING BACK ON CHILDHOOD

The fifties and sixties are seen as pivotal years in world, Irish and local history. Those decades saw major changes in all aspects of life from work to music. But there were smaller things about that era.

IMPS: These were not the creatures of legend but sweets. They were small and black and came in boxes smaller than matchboxes. They were called sweets but although they looked like liquorice they were hot, hot, hot. They were not little devils but they probably singed the taste buds of a generation.

TAWS: Called marbles by the more genteel were the Olympics of the school

Mellow Candle—A four-piece group from Dublin. This is the only unknown group in the Festival. They have not made any records to date but it is hoped that after their performance in Wexford their name will be more widely known.

CONCERT PROGRAMME

Thursday, March 18th :

Abbey Cinema—Danny Doyle, The Johnstons, The Strawbs.

Friday, March 19th :

Theatre Royal—Benthein Quartet; Scarabrae; The Chieftians, Maire Nic Shinn.

Abbey Cinema—Southern Comfort; Curved Air.

Saturday, March 20th :

Theatre Royal—R.T.E. String Quartet; John Beckett; New Irish Chamber Orchestra.

Dun Mhuire—Mellow Candle; Tir Na Nog; Principal Edwards Magic Theatre.

Sunday, March 21st :

Abbey Cinema—Dr. Strangely Strange; Fairport Convention.

Right: A newspaper cutting reminds us of the 1971 line up at the Festival of Living Music.

Below: A delighted audience at a concert that may or may not be part of the Festival of Living Music.

playground or any bit of waste ground. Like the Olympics there were numerous types of event. The more conventional had a circle scratched in the earth with each player placing a taw – a glass sphere about half inch diameter with coloured leaves inside – on the line. It was best if each could have a different colour. Then the players lined up a set distance from the ring and propelled another taw by means of a sophisticated flick of the thumb towards the ring. Knocking a taw out of the ring meant that the player kept it. After each in turn had 'fired' they continued playing on like golf, 'firing' towards the ring from wherever the taw settled. Landing in the ring meant returning to the start.

In taws there were serious offences. 'Run the Knuckle' occurred when players got closer to the target with some unscrupulous people moving the hand forward as they 'fired' thus gaining unfair distance. An offence by outsiders was called 'chickling' whereby some canat ran up, scooped up the taws and ran off.

Variation on the taws theme included 'Taw in the Hole' where a small hole was dug and the game was played like a poor mans snooker with the idea being to knock taws into the hole with another taw. A version without a name helped shorten the walk from school as two people propelled taws along the street hitting each other's taw in turn.

LUCKY LUMPS: These were lumps of sweet usually red on the outside and white inside. The were about an inch either way in dimensions and on biting into the hard sweet, a proportion of people found a three penny bit – hence the name.

LOOSE BISCUITS: In the pre pre-packaging days, biscuits were sold from tins in the shops. Initially the tins were kept on high shelves and as varieties were limited it was quite simple to ask for your half pound of Marietta or Arrowroot (these for some reason were bought and fed to canaries). With the increase in varieties the tins were fitted with glass lids and placed at counter level to tempt the purchaser and there was often a self-service element provided you didn't want to mix chocolate biscuits and plain ones.

An important social side effect of this practice was 'broken biscuits'. No one wanted to put broken biscuits out on the Sunday table so anyone buying them took only the complete items. This left boxes with many half and quarter biscuits so shopkeepers established a practice of lumping these together and offering reduced price 'broken biscuits'. This meant more for your money and a wider choice per bag.

The early packets of biscuits were four old pennies and usually had 8 or ten biscuits of a single variety wrapped in a greaseproof paper pack. 'Nice' were probably one of the best. Glossy coloured wrappers came later with 'USA Assorted' being the top one, usually purchased for special visitors and later for Sunday tea.

TIG or TAG: Another street and school playground game was tig. There was a variation on tig to suit every mood, grouping and location. Tig Hunt was probably the original. It meant one or two people being picked to chase and catch members of the larger group with the last one or two caught then being 'on it' or being the chasers.

Like all games there was ritual. The choosing of whoever was 'on it' probably resembled the ancient rituals of the Celts in choosing human sacrifice. All participants were lined up in a straight line or circle. Then a chosen one 'gave it out'. This meant pointing to each in turn while reciting any one of a number of incantations.

'Eeny, meeny, miney, moe catch the babby by the toe, if he squeals let him go.

Eeny, meeny, miney moe'. Each word had a different person pointed to and on the final 'moe' either that person was 'on it' or free depending on the rules used. If the latter the incantation was repeated until only one person remained and they were 'it'. 'Inkey pinkey pen and inkey you go out because you're stinkey' was another rhyme.

Having decided sides the gang had to get a chance to hide. To accomplish this the chasers had to 'hide their eyes'. This meant not looking for a count to 100 usually done in fives – five, ten, fifteen, twenty.....

Major feats of athletics were witnessed on streets in a game of tig. Hedges were leaped, banks were slid down, and cars were dodged as everyone tried to avoid being touched by the chasers. Anyone touched was deemed caught and had to sit out the rest of the game. There were of course other rules and regulations. Boundaries were set within which the game was played and anyone going outside these was deemed caught. Players could call 'tax' and cross their fingers in which case they were given a 'dar'. This could only be used in extreme cases such as getting hurt or being called by 'the mammy'.

Tig Den was a variation on Chase. In this as well as avoiding capture, one was required to try to touch 'den', a designated windowsill, schoolbag, rock, coat or something. If touched you were safe and would not be caught to be 'on it' in the next game.

Tig In was another sub species. In this anyone caught was required to stand near a wall with one arm outstretched touching the wall. Any brave soul could then run under the arms and free those caught.

Tig On was a continuous game. In this the person touched became the chaser and so the game could continue until people got tired of it.

Tig Sticky was a variation of Tig On but the person touched had to hold the part of the body touched while they chased the others. Touching the ankle could produce an interesting chaser.

THE IRELAND'S OWN STORY

Much is written and said about the major periodicals of the world – *Reader' Digest*, *National Geographic*, *The Bell* and others, but here in Wexford we have a weekly magazine that has been a continuous best seller since 1902. The Walsh family, proprietors of *The People* Newspaper, established *Ireland's Own*, just after the start of the twentieth century. Their intention was to provide an Irish alternative to English magazines such as *John O' London's Weekly* and *Titbits*. Both of these have long since departed but *Ireland's Own* lives on.

Within the first decade it was attracting letters from Portugal, Canada, Buenos Aires and Bombay, and continues to do so. It's early subtitle - *A Journal of Fiction Literature and General Information* - aptly described its contents that were eagerly sought after by an increasingly literate population at home and abroad.

In that first decade it published articles on Holiday Resorts, Racing, Fashion, Etiquette, Cookery, Trivia as well as short stories, a serial and a Gaelic language column. In 1911 books in the Ireland's Own Library series were printed, usually enlarged versions of serials by the likes of Desmond Lough and Victor O'Donovan Power. 22 July 1914 saw the debut of a fictional character that was to remain popular throughout the century - Kitty the Hare. That same year witnessed a maritime disaster off Fethard, County Wexford that was to draw condolences from around the world, through the columns of *Ireland's Own*.

The advent of The Great War cast shadows over every aspect of Irish life, including *Ireland's Own*. So too did national events. The 'recent upheaval in Dublin' as the editor put it in May 1916 caused two issues of *Ireland's Own* to be lost, due to fires destroying paper stocks. Near the end of its second decade another fire caused a break in publication and a change of printer that resulted in a new magazine size and altered headings. That was in February 1922. The 1920s were years of change. Cinema going was on the increase and *Ireland's Own* reflected this in articles like *Secrets of Cinemaland*. Graphology, legal queries, fortune telling, gramophone reviews and a shopping service were also introduced.

Thirty years after its foundation, *Ireland's Own* was back being printed in Wexford, having transferred to Dublin for a time, but its outlook remained national. Various Irish towns were featured in its pages. Photos from the latest films were printed. Cartoons were introduced and An Oige provided a regular column. The Second World War caused the magazine to be reduced to 16 pages per issue, due to paper shortages. Yet it was in the middle of those war years that the now famous 'Pen Friends' began as a short column in April 1943 - the humble beginnings of countless friendships.

The start of Aer Rianta's transatlantic flights was celebrated with a special issue. This led to photos being used on the covers on a regular basis, ranging from scenery to puzzle pictures. The 1950s covers featured line drawings of Irish landscapes and townscapes, which advertised the charms of various districts to a population growing increasingly mobile.

As ever, *Ireland's Own* reflected the wishes and interests of Irish readers, at home and abroad. The best of its early features shared page space with the latest innovations. But it remained the magazine for every member of the family. Through the decades this continued. Covers changed. Special issues were produced - Halloween, St Valentines Day, Humour Annuals, Songbooks and Short Story Annuals took their place beside the long established St Patrick's Day and Christmas specials.

In the 1980s colour pictures became regular features on the covers of *Ireland's Own*. In 1988 two special editions were to attract great praise. The Dublin Millennium and even more, the Australian Bicentennial editions were hailed as some of the best commemorative publications of the events. Approaching a century of publication, *Ireland's Own* continues the hopes of its founding family. It is a true family magazine. It is an Irish alternative of foreign publications. It is not a woman's magazine, it is not a religious magazine, it is not a joke book, it is not a songbook, it is not a comic, it is not a literary magazine, but in a way it is all of these.

Through the years, *Ireland's Own* has been the voice of the people of Ireland at home and abroad. It has given an outlet to their writing and it has preserved the best of our songs and stories. It has travelled from a back street in Wexford to all parts of the world.

A LITTLE THEATRE IN WEXFORD

The Theatre Royal was the brainchild of a local newspaper owner over 150 years ago. Mr. William Taylor was proprietor and editor of the *Wexford Herald* when work began on the theatre in 1830. On completion it was leased to a Mr. McGowan of Belfast and it was under his management that the Theatre Royal first opened its doors on 4 January in 1832.

The first artistes to grace its boards were Mr. Daly and Miss Graham. The performance began at 7.30 and patrons paid the rather expensive sum of three shillings for a box, two shillings in the pit and one shilling in the gallery. In its early days, lighting was by candle and oil lamps and the Theatre Royal attracted large crowds from all over the county. So large were these crowds that there are reports of the streets surrounding the theatre being blocked with carriages of patrons.

Unfortunately, large crowds were not a constant and for a short period the theatre closed, becoming an auction room and later a lending library. Thankfully, this was but a minor setback and performers were soon back on the stage, with a mixture of comedy, drama and general entertainment. Apparently, Wexford people took their drama quite seriously in those days and a rather interesting story circulates about one particular performance. The play concerned was *The Colleen Bawn* and at one point it is said that a local sailor had to be physically restrained to prevent him leaping from the balcony to rescue the heroine. Not that all of the drama occurred within the theatre. A newspaper report of May 1835 recalls a publicity stunt for a show being performed at the Theatre Royal where a pantomime clown was towed down the river Slaney in a washtub harnessed to two geese.

An advertisement in the Wexford Chronicle for December 31st 1832 tells us that Romeo & Juliet was to be performed by permission of the mayor, performance to start at 7.30 (bell will not be rung in future), box 3/=, pit 2/=, gallery 1/=.

In 1889 Miss Tellier's Dramatic Co. presented the Octoroon. With the advent of films, the theatre was refurbished and for some years it divided its facilities between films and live shows. In 1902 – 'For three nights only with matinee on Saturday at 3.00, seats (reserved) 3/= each at Mr. Sinnott's, 29 South Main Street. The Original Irish Company will present the world renowned Edison Animated Pictures witnessed by the Lord Lieutenant, clergy of all denominations, John Redmond and 250,000 people at Rotunda, Dublin. Pronounced by press as Perfection of Animated Photography. Including: Life in Ireland; National Convention; Punchestown Races; Cork Exhibition; Spring Show; Little Tich; Tally Ho; President McKinley Funeral; Across the Atlantic; Niagara Falls; 500 humorous, mystical and up to date pictures; Archbishop Croke's Funeral; Coronation; Stag Hunt at Punchestown. Open 7.30, commences 8.00, carriages 10.15.' The last item there was a handy hint to let the lackeys know that the boss would be finished at the pictures at a quarter past ten so the best get the carriages up to High Street.

In the same year 'Miss Bessie Lesta's Grand Combination Company of American, Continental and Japanese Artistes with Craig, Raze and Craig - Silver Bar and Trapeze Artistes, premier grotesques and musical clowns, jugglers and performing pigeons and male impersonators. Reserved seats 3/=, boxes 2/=, pit 1/=, gallery 6d.' Lloyds Mexican Circus offered; a football match on bicycles, the goodnight horse, clowns and two dudes, plus Edison Norton Cinematograph. On 25 November 1906 a new comedy *To Marry or Not To Marry* along with *My Grandmother* was billed. Mr. and Mrs. Lacy of Theatre Royal Covent Garden and Mr. & Mrs. Neyler of Theatre Royal Crowe Street with some others would appear.

'Do your Christmas shopping in Theatre Royal Café – wines, Sherries, sweets' was an advertisement in 1945.

Not that all of the live shows were strictly entertainment. A series entitled The Gilchrist Lecture were given in the Theatre Royal early in this century. The theme was 'Science for the People' and the lecturers actually went around the local factories drumming up support and seeking promises of attendance. But comedy and drama were the most popular entertainments. International troupes like the Globe Theatre Company from London shared stage time with the KKK or Koloured Komedy Kompany who used Ks instead of Cs in their title and who performed pantomimes and musicals. The Theatre Royal was the venue for Wexford's first bi-lingual pantomime in 1946 when Smeachoidin or Cinderella was performed.

Some years later, the theatre, which had such humble beginnings, became home to a dream. Some Wexfordmen had the idea of organising a festival where little known works of opera would be given a wider audience. The dream took hold, audiences from around the world heard about this little festival, in a little theatre in a little town in Ireland. They came to find out more, they were captivated by everything about the idea and the world famous Wexford Festival of Opera grew in the little theatre. The Theatre Royal also attracts names like Mary Black, Billy Connolly and Phil Coulter as well as the young stars of opera.

Another attraction of the Theatre Royal is one seldom seen. He is the theatre ghost, Johnny Hoey and he is said to get rather upset if the last person to leave the theatre forgets to say goodbye.

NOT SO ANCIENT HISTORY

History for is not Brian Boru and hundreds of years ago. It is ordinary people and last year or twenty years ago. One of those ordinary people of history was the late Wally Doyle PC. In a simple, unplanned conversation over a pint, Wally could give a greater insight into our past than many professors.

On one such occasion he spoke of the card schools held every Sunday night at his family's farmhouse at Whiterock in Wexford. A large group of family, friends and neighbours gathered in the large kitchen that was situated between the parlour and the 'wake room', and settled in for a long nights entertainment. To aid their pleasure, the children would have spent the afternoon rolling up strips of Saturday nights Evening Herald into tapers. These were placed in a jam jar in the centre of the table and used to light the pipes from the open grate.

On other Sunday evenings people calling to the farm to collect milk would seat themselves near the house and await the arrival of Mister Ennis. He was the gardener at the Rectory on Spawell Road and was a very well read man. His Sunday evening role was that of dramatic reader. A hush would come over the group as he sat down, donned his steel rimmed glasses and picked up the previous evenings paper. Then with dramatic pauses and variations of accent he would read the weekly serial instalment. One of the joys of listening to people like Wally was the way one topic leads seamlessly into another one, which is totally unrelated.

From dramatic readers he moved on to weddings in the war years. He told of guests giving their ration coupons for tea, sugar and butter to be served at the reception to the caterer. The bride and groom often purchased ration coupons for clothes in order to be able to get new clothes or a 'rig out' as it was called, for the wedding. The wedding ceremony itself was usually performed before 7 am mass and for most people it was on a side altar of the church, the main altar being reserved for upper class nuptials. This early ceremony led to the wedding meal being referred to as a wedding breakfast.

Weddings and caterers led to talk of apprentices. Apprentices were paid a pittance as they worked to learn a trade. The work was hard, the hours long and overtime payment was unheard of. A young girl apprenticed to the confectionery trade might

Wexford Quay shows ships of sail. (Lawrence Collection)

start her day by lighting the oven at 4 am and continue work well into the evening. If after such a long day she had the energy to socialise, it had to be short lived as a live in apprentice returning home after 10 pm could well find herself locked out.

Somehow the conversation went from bakeries to cattle. He recalled the busy days of Wexford port, of the City of Cork Steam Packet Company ship The Blarney berthing at the quay. There it took on live cattle that had been driven down from the company cattle yard half a mile away. He smiled as he reminded me of the possible state of the quays on sailing day. Recalling such seemingly mundane events makes one realise the richness of the history that is passing and should remind us to preserve the memories of not just our grandparents and parents but also our own.

SAILING

Blue seas, bright sunshine and billowing sails are our usual view of the sailor's life on the brigs, square-riggers and schooners of times past. This is partly caused by television and films and of course our own perception of that luxury cruise. In reality, life on board those romantic ships was far from the stuff of fantasy.

To begin with, we must realise that the sailing ships were not pleasure craft. They were commercial undertakings, every bit as profit driven as the sweatshops, mines and factories. Ship owners were businessmen whose aim in life was to make money, not to be a philanthropist. We should also bear in mind that the sailing ships of our dreams sailed more often from Wexford, Cardiff or Bantry than from Tahiti or Samoa. This meant sailing more often in showers than in sunshine, as for example it is recorded in the log of the brig 'Alert' sailing from Wexford in July of 1866:

'Friday 6th – Towed out of dock. Squally with rane (rain), thunder and lightning. Got the gib boom out and studding sails on the yards'.

And remember this was in July. Imagine a voyage beginning in November or December. The weather in those days was no better nor worse than it is today, but if sailing was planned, sailing took place or else the sailors were not paid. Our perception of life on board ship is also based on misconceptions. We see all sailing ships as sorts of ocean going liners with plenty of room and private cabins. The vast majority of sailors in the 1800s shipped aboard vessels little bigger than the trawlers seen to-day in any fishing port.

As for space, this was at a premium. The less space occupied by a crewman, the greater the capacity to carry cargo and the higher the profit. Most sailors had little more than the space of the bunk he occupied as a place of privacy, and many of these were used on a sort of time share basis, with someone else bunking down in one mans bed while he was on watch. Remember that there was always at least one person on duty, keeping an eye out for ships or other hazards.

In general, ships watches were of 4 hours duration, with 4 hours off, ostensibly to rest and possibly sleep but most skippers had other ideas on how such time was spent.

Life on a sailing ship was not confined to gazing at the horizon and hauling sail. When not involved in the actual task of sailing a ship, which was most of the voyage time, sailors were put to work at various jobs. Maintenance of a sailing ship was carried out while under sail whenever possible. All painting, including over the sides were 'off watch' occupations as was sail repair and of course scrubbing the decks.

Food on board ship is another of our modern movie inspired fantasies. We tend as always to think of *The Bounty* and its exotic fruits. Sailing from an Irish port on a locally owned ship gave little chance of coconuts or breadfruits. Most owners provisioned their ships either from their own merchant stores or from their farms. This led to a rather variable fare depending on the resources and generosity of the shipowner. In those days there was no refrigeration and so the life of certain goods could be rather short. In general, the sailors ate rather well on the first days of the voyage when vegetables and other perishables were still fresh.

A typical menu for a sailor might consist of the following: -

> 7.30 am Breakfast - some meat left over from the previous day, tea and biscuits (more on these below).
> 12.30 Dinner - half a pound of meat (pork or beef on alternate days, which were pickled to preserve them), vegetables (when available) and potatoes (while they lasted).
> 5.00 p.m. Tea - a repeat of the breakfast menu.

The biscuits referred to were not chocolate digestives or even plain digestives. Their official name was Water Biscuits but they were variously known as 'blahs' or ' pantiles'. Each man had a ration of these daily from the captain or the cook. To begin with this might be one pond per day, but as stocks dwindled the amount could drop. It is generally agreed that these biscuits were far from luxury items. They were hard as rocks and usually came with their own assortment of maggots, weevils and other creatures. In order to eat these biscuits, it is reported that they were put into a canvas bag and pounded with iron bars, both to kill the insects and to make the food eatable. The crumbs were mixed with water into a kind of gruel for consumption.

Some owners gave little extras like pots of marmalade or pounds of butter at regular intervals and these were added to the mashed biscuits.

From the ships log of *The Alert* we can gain some idea of the provisions carried on a typical sailing ship. In 1866 these included corn, eggs, potatoes, cabbage and onions. In Constantinople they also took on board some 'soft bread' and one case of gin.

Other items from the log indicate the occupations of men on the voyage. Sail needles were purchased, as were fishhooks and paint.

The old refrain of 'water water everywhere and ne'er a drop to drink' also proved very true for the sailors of the 1800s. As stated previously, space on board ship was limited and cargo space was given priority. This meant that only a limited amount of fresh water was carried and this was carefully rationed. In one recorded case the ration was 2 quarts per man per day. From this he had to give a certain amount to the cook to cover his cooking needs. The remainder was closely guarded and was usually kept on the sailor's person throughout the day. As may be imagined such a small amount of water meant that washing was rather difficult, while living in such close proximity made it essential. To overcome the problem, each man put a measured amount into a basin and then they drew lots to determine turns taken for washing. On longer voyages when heavy rain in warm climates was encountered, most men stripped off and had a good wash. Conversely, a voyage through particularly bad weather could mean 24 a day, 7 days a week encased in oilskins.

Living and working for long periods under such conditions often led to conflict and sometimes desertion. Anyone who deserted or 'jumped ship' forfeited any belongings left behind and wages due. If caught up with later, he was also liable for the cost of his replacement. Such replacement was of the utmost importance as not ship carried excess crewmen, so if one man left another had to be found to take his place or else

These wooden steps gave access to the rowing boats. (Rossiter Collection)

considerable burdens were placed on the remaining crew.

Crewmen were also lost through natural or accidental death. Life on board ship was hard and often quite dangerous. Sails had to be stowed or unfurled in all sorts of weather and it all seas from calm to stormy and even the most sure-footed seaman could make a fatal mistake.

When such a tragedy occurred, the skipper took charge of all of his possessions, money and clothing. These were brought home to his relatives. If there were no relatives, the goods were auctioned either among the crew or back in port, and the proceeds were given to a group called the Trustees for the Relief of Seamen. All of this was laid down in regulations and a complete inventory was kept in the ships log.

Such a log, gives us a true picture of the belongings of a nineteenth century sailor.

'James Edwards drowned while furling the top main sail, despite all efforts to save him. Belongings: 2 flannel shirts, 1 singlet, 2 caps, 2 pair of trousers, 2 pocket handkerchiefs, 1 pair of stockings, 1 pipe, 1 blanket, 1 bed box, tin box with 5 pictures.

Signed Luke Shiels (Master); Thomas Rowe (Mate) 1/8/1864.'

Another aspect of the sailor's life to remember is that it was not only at sea that he worked. The 1800s saw very little mechanisation at ports and all loading and unloading of the ships was done by crewmembers, sometimes with the assistance of others.

The Alert carried 360 tons of coal from Cardiff to Malta and the crew spent five days in sweltering Mediterranean heat discharging it.

Despite the hardships, the sea and sailing was a major source of employment in the 1800s. Boys went to sea at the age of 12 as apprentices. These were taken on to learn the trade of seamanship, but were often little more than unpaid labour. In some areas, boys destined for the Workhouse were sent instead to sea as apprentices. In the more established ports, it was the sons of sailors who took these apprenticeship places, thus carrying on family traditions.

THE 'FAIR DO'
(A song of the Rosslare Regatta, 1940)

On the eighteenth of August in this present year
The Fair Do and her crew down to Rosslare did steer.
The wind it was high, but the weather was grand,
And the view of the race was tip-top from the strand.

We left the Fair Do at the Pier Head one night,
And to our surprise she was "their" delight.
They moulded her model and measured her mast,
And said, 'tween themselves, "Let us build one as fast."

The Pier and Rosslare men were there in their cots;
The big bugs were sailing around in their yachts.
But the crowd down from Wexford all gave a hurroo
When they saw Eddie Daly try out the Fair Do.

When we went to get measured we all got a fright,
The bloke at the job would not pull the tape tight.
"Twenty-one feet three inches," he shouted out clear;
She'd stretched five inches more since we sailed to the Pier.

The Spitfire's coxswain he got a bit hot
When he saw the Fair Do overhauling his cot.
He hauled twice across us, said "I won't let you out,"
But we bid him good-bye when we hove her about.

When we got to the windward, oh, boys, it was grand
To see the Fair Do beating in to the strand.
When we turned the last buoy and the home way was clear,
The Spitfire still had her head to the Pier.

He lodged an objection soon after the race,
Although his 'fast' cot could not take second place.

We'll meet him again when we'll saw her in two,
And bring back the cup in the clipper, 'Fair Do.

And now I will tell you the names of the crew:
Eddie Daly, John Walsh and his brother, Jim, too.
When they sailed past the flag-boat the cheering was great,
And the Spitfire passed it four minutes too late

When they brought her ashore and stepped out on the strand
The lads down from Wexford shook them all by the hand.
It was a great race boys, but between me and you,
I doubt they had steam in the clipper Fair Do.

This ballad, sung to the air of "Cod Liver Oil,"

This is the boat The Fair Do. It was the subject of a ballad in Songs of the Wexford coast after a great but contentious regatta victory in 1944. (Rossiter Collection)

This would have been a typical scene at dinnertime or closing time at Pierces although this was probably posed. The date is 1939. (Pierce Centenary Booklet – John Rossiter)

PIERCES – STORY AND CONNECTIONS

Wexford is not regarded as a factory town, such as the ones dominated by the dark satanic mills of English literature. But parts of the town and its inhabitants were factory dominated. It is only when we look back without the rose tinted spectacles that we remember the reality of how the factory overshadowed portions of Wexford.

The original Pierce Company started in 1839 at Kilmore making fire fans, an improvement on the bellows, which soon became familiar fittings in homes throughout the country. With expansion into agricultural machinery Pierce moved into Wexford, to the Mill Road Works, as this property is properly called. The name Mill Road derives from Richard Devereux's Flour Mill, one of the largest in Ireland, which stood in the south eastern section of the complex, on the Mulgannon Road, In 1856 Pierces got the contract to build a bridge across the Slaney at Carcur. In order to execute this contract the firm devised and built their own machines for use on the project. The railings of the bridge, designed and made by Wexfordmen could still be seen over 150 years later at the cattle mart site on Redmond Road, almost oppos te the old bridge location. The foundries products were sold worldwide. They had offices and showrooms in Paris and Buenos Aires in the late nineteenth century. From the French capital Mr. P erce imported a Tontine Society idea, of working men saving a small sum regularly towards occasions such as Christmas. But more importantly, on the death of a member of the group, all contributed a fixed sum towards the burial of the deceased. This system relieved the minds of people haunted by the prospect of interment in a pauper's grave. This Pierce innovation was to spread from the factory's soc al club on Paul Quay to almost every street in Wexford. During the F rst World War P erces was used as a munitions factory, with local women working during the day and the men carrying on shifts through the night. A newspaper report of the period gives a flavour of the work and dangers, 'Ellen Leary of The Faythe working at Pierces

70

Here we see workers leaving a much diminished Pierce's in the 1980s. (Rossiter Collection)

Munitions Factory was cleaning her machine when her hand was caught in the cogs. Her finger was crushed. A lorry was requisitioned to bring her to County Infirmary. Dr O'Connor treated her.' The company also produced bicycles at this time, some of wh ch surv ve to this day. With the recession of the mid-1960s Pierces began a series of reductions of staff and changes of ownership. The company since closed.

In general Pierces did not monopolise but did dominate people and areas of the town. As a major employer this was inevitable. The Lockout of 1911 is well documented and shows the effect of the foundries on Wexford life in all its aspects from work to religion to social interaction. But it was not in disputes that this dominance – predominantly benign – was evident. Even as it peaked and began to dwindle Pierces was a major force in very many lives. In the 1950s our lives were, if not ruled, at least very influenced by that powerful siren which marked the start and end of the working day. For those who never experienced it, the sound was like the air raid siren of the movies and was activated, in the 1950s, at 8 am, 12.30 and 1.30 for lunch start and end and perhaps 5.30 pm.

For anyone passing the factory at 12.30 or 5.30 it was like witnessing a grand prix start as pedestrians and cyclists poured out the gates before the siren echo had died.

Not that the working day was strictly within those hours. Night work and overtime were very common in that decade. It was not unusual for children returning from school to meet their father or Da for tea and before they started their homework to get the 'Slan Leat' as he left for the night shift. Working overtime often led to adventure for the children. Canteens and even thermos flasks were not as common in those days so the Ma sent down the billycan and sandwiches around 5.30.

The child's first port of call was to 'the office' where Johnny Byrne was often on duty to grant permission to enter. Johnny was a sort of security man before the days

71

of uniforms and walkie-talkies. If the child were new to the factory, Johnny would accompany them to the Da or take the grub in for them. The older 'hands' were permitted to enter the foundry themselves if they were sure where they were going.

In Pierce's you needed to know where you were going and to be very careful. This was a huge factory covering acres and with very may potentially dangerous operations in progress.

My Da worked as a welder. His place of work could be reached via the yard or up through the forge. I usually preferred the Forge route especially when my grandfather was working there as foreman. He was Nicky, always called as 'The Da' as distinct from my Da who was called Nicky. I was called Nicholas.

The forge was a place I can still recall from the sounds and smells. It was a huge shed with a number of fires. The predominant sound was the clank of steel and the smells were coke and heat. The Da as foreman was always dressed in a brown 'shop coat' and felt hat with a pen protruding from the top pocket.

The welding shop as it was called, was a cordoned off area at the top of the forge. Here the smell was sort of ozone, scorched air. Me Da was a figure in dungarees with a welding mask and a welding rod like sparklers 'fizzing' in his hand. His co-workers were Paddy Curran and Hopper McGrath, a popular hurler on the county team.

Pierces was very much a factory where families worked. I had an uncle who was foreman in the Paint Shop and another who worked in either the Moulding Shop or the Edge Tool. The Moulding Shop was where moulds were made in a sort of sandstone into which metal was poured. The Edge Tool Shop was where tools, spades, sprongs, scythes etc with sharp edges were manufactured. The tea delivery run was a special time for youngsters. It brought us into the world of work, the magic of the factory, meeting the men. It was magic and probably encouraged many to go into that line of employment.

Life was also about play and Pierces dominated this by default. To be blunt about it we played on a slagheap of waste from the factory. To us it was an adventure playground, Disneyland and a movie set. The Knock, as it was known, was the dumping ground for lorry loads of waste from Pierces driven in those days by Hughie Doyle. The land was a large area adjoining the former site of the Bishopswater Distillery. It extended out to what was then the country and it was 'heaven'.

The Knock had a river – The Horse River- a bridge, enclosed banks, exposed banks, an old garage, the remains of the distillery storage bunkers, the factory dump, bramble bushes, furze, a road and a tunnel.

The Horse River was also known as the Bishopswater River. It fed the distillery in its day and also powered the wheels of Pierces downriver. In the 1950s the lower end was paved and the upper end had various manufactured dams or weirs. For now I will concentrate on the area within the Knock. Flow in this river varied with weather and seasons. In flood it would overrun its banks often to depths of 12 or 15 feet. In summer it was often a stinking trickle with a plentiful supply of rates scurrying about.

The river was a great attraction and caused many a wet foot and much more as we fell – usually backwards – into it's none too sparkling water. One weird pastime I recall involved sheets of galvanized roofing. For some reason we put this in the water and then stood like a surfer on it, rocking it to make waves.

Building dams was another popular pastime, which kept us busy and wet for weeks.

The bridge over the river was a concrete affair, which stood at least 20 feet above the water. I cannot recall anyone falling from this potentially very dangerous structure. Our primary use for it other than as a route to other areas was for dropping rocks, sods and anything else into the river.

Less than 20 metres from the bridge was 'the tunnel'. This was the Holy Grail, the test, the place we half feared half loved. The Tunnel was the test. Could you go down this dark river cavern of a few hundred yards? It was the place of myth. There were stories of rooms leading off it and stretching for miles. Unfortunately they were just stories. The tunnel was man made to route the river under the Casa Rio houses. The only dangers were the ever-present rats and the very definite possibility of falling on your behind in the river. Still, it was an adventure, which tested many a nerve as expeditions worthy of Indiana Jones – decades before he appeared – set off into that lost world under mountains of earth and the old garage.

The garage – we are not sure what it really was – was a huge roofless building at the bottom of the Knock opposite Willie Goodison's shop. At one time the wooden gates were intact and it had to be climbed into. Then the gates went and the adventure of getting into the Garage was diminished. There was a lingering dare. Some of the old roof beams managed to survive and the stouthearted among us sometimes ventured out along the rotting timbers 30 feet above the rubble-strewn floor.

Outside The Garage a number of concrete lintels were strewn about. Some seemed to young eyes to form an airplane and so was used for that purpose. On another side, a stepped area was our stagecoach.

Beyond the Garage was the next step in adventure – the route to The Tank. The Tank was our name for the rack and concrete vault, which we believed, once held the whiskey of Bishopswater Distillery. It was more likely a storage facility. The path to the Tank went behind and far above the rear of Casa Rio houses. At one point a 6-inch ledge with a 30-degree slope had to be negotiated and added greatly to the adventure. From here we looked down on the sad remnants of the distillery.

Yet another section of The Knock was The Plantation. This was in a number of sections all wired off from the main area. It comprised of steep banks on which trees were planted for Arbour Day in about 1950. They were for the most part grass and furze covered areas and were occasionally set ablaze in summer months. At night they took on a new role. It was another testing ground as groups braved the dark trails and heard tales of "The White Lady".

Another part of the Knock was The Bank. This was the route to school – it halved the journey. The Bank was a combination of routes. The most popular was so used that the grass was long since worn away and the soil greatly eroded. In dry weather it was relatively safe with rudimentary steps cut into the clay – yellow – at times. As weather got very dry there was a problem with trying to climb in dust. Going home there were the walkers and those who ran down the Bank.

Wet weather transformed The Bank into a minor waterfall or gorge with a stream of water and sludgy mud. But still we often braved it. The alternative was to go slightly to the left and climb up in the wet grass. There were more footholds and sods to pull on but it was a much wetter route. The third way was to use a sort of drainage area still further to the left. This was sort of stepped and because it was less used did not get quite so muddy. Either way on a cold wet windy day the odds were always stacked on getting a muddy behind as you slip slid and bounced down the Bank but that was

73

life. The flat area of the Knock and the slopes down to the river behind Alvina Brook were also furze covered with trails and routes that could be Kansas or Germany or a 101 other film scenes. It was a truly marvelous place in the 1950s and 1960s. It was an industrial dump, but we saw only the land of dreams. The road for Hughie Doyle in that grey lorry was the main route. Between chest high furze bushes imaginary horses were galloped and GI's of 10 years of age 'belly-crawled' for hours. The dumping area itself must have contained millions of tons of debris. We only saw the edge as a dumping area where metal shavings, sand moulds, lumps of steel, coke and a zillion other things were deposited. At that edge the dump rose 10 or 12 feet above a grassed area to become level with the 'real' Knock so we must assume that the Knock was the result of feet of waste atop an original field. The metal shavings were extraordinary. They formed silvery mattresses onto which we jumped. These were often about 10 square feet and 2 feet thick. Remember this was shaved steel – probably razor sharp but we played on it. Not that we always escaped injury. Throwing various shaped stones and pieces of metal had its dangers. I recall on one occasion throwing a piece of metal then looking at my hand. The little finger of the right hand had a slit about one inch long. I could see the green-yellow finger bone. I honestly believe that I covered the distance of about 500 yards from tip to home at such speed that I hardly lost a drop of blood.

John O'Connor was not so lucky in another one of our famous 'sod fight'. These usually took place down near the gate and basically we threw sods at each other. On that particular day I can still 'see' John. A sod hit him directly in the face so he was clay covered. Unfortunately there must have been a piece of slate or metal in the sod because, within seconds, streams of blood flowed from the top of his head over his face. Thankfully it was not a serious injury – I still marvel at how trivial any of our injuries ever were. I cannot recall a major accident in the Knock.

This is a picture of one of the fountains in front of the houses on Avenue de Flandres. The walled land on the right belonged to Cromwell's Fort.

(Pierce Centenary Book –John Rossiter)

Like all dumping grounds, The Knock began to attract domestic rubbish and this provided areas where we seldom went, as there were always rats around them.

Rats were endemic in the area and the gardens of Alvina Brook were regularly invaded so poison, traps and air guns were common. I recall a story of Mrs. Browne at number 9 who caught a rat in the trap. She got her son's pellet rifle and spent some time trying to kill the creature by shooting it in the behind. Mention has already been made of Alvina Brook and Casa Rio. These, along with Avenue de Flandres were groups of houses built by Pierces for senior and junior staff members to whom they were rented.

Casa Rio was a very unusual row of terraced house. Four of them are accessed via short bridges from road to front door, over the Horse River, which flows about 12 feet below. The other houses are even more interesting. In these, the front hallway forms this bridge over the river. In the rear there is a service road that enters at a point near the old Distillery and runs behind the houses dividing the gardens from the back yards. Being built over the river, they have often suffered flooding at times when the river rose to window level. Casa Rio (House on the river) houses were occupied in the main by middle management.

Foremen more often rented Alvina Brook houses. These were similar to Casa Rio but were smaller and single storey. A distinctive feature was the arched porch and red brick surrounds. The porches of Alvina Brook were echoed by a covered spring or spout opposite Casa Rio. This facility with the legend 'Aqua Pura' inscribed above it was a source of water during summer months when the municipal supply was either tainted or depleted. There was a steady stream of bucket carrying people trying to pick the least busy time to call down. For most of my memory the spout as we called it was flooded and there were stepping-stones inside. It also had two stone seats inside.

Avenue de Flandres was the estate for the higher management echelon. It was a row of houses build atop a hill overlooking the factory and Casa Rio. There were gates either end of the estate and a very steep incline from the Casa Rio side. Avenue de Flandres took its name from the address of Pierces office in Paris. They also had an office in Buenos Aires. The houses fronted onto two fountains and midway down the hill there was an artificial pond wither side of the road with a connecting tunnel.

This pond was a magnet for young people from the area. The big attraction was the tadpoles, but there were also roacheens and bardoges. Jam jars and nets made of wire and pieces of old nylon stockings were the norm. Some had real store bought nets. The children were usually tolerated at this pond but venturing up the hill to the fountains was seen as daring. Huge Cypress trees flanked the hill. Between Willie Goodison's and the avenue was a wasteland of briar, bog and 'yella marl' which was yet another adventure playground. Pierces also had a store on the quays where Joyce's is now.

GONE IN 40 YEARS

Looking back to the commercial life of Wexford in the late 1960s it is startling to recall how many of the 'names' of that era are gone. Some were amalgamated, some moved, some changed name.

ACCOUNTANTS
Brandon, Ferguson & Co. The Bullring
Deevy W. A. & Co The Bullring
Hodnett & Co. 36 Selskar Street

THIS WEEK'S BARGAINS!

NURSERY BEDROOM SUITE, ... £9 9 0
WALNUT AND MAHOGANY DINING-ROOM TABLES from £3 3 0
BEDS in Rosewood and Mahogany from £10 10 0

These are a few of the many

to be had at

₋owney's

Peter Street and Henrietta St., Wexford
SATISFACTION GUARANTEED.

This advertisement dates from the early days of a family business that grew with Wexford.

Important Sale of well-known Hotel and Business Premises.

TO BE SOLD BY AUCTION

At the Chamber of Commerce,
WEXFORD.

On Wednesday, 22nd day of March, 1922
AT THE HOUR OF TWO O'CLOCK.
BY DIRECTIONS OF MR TIMOTHY BYRNE.
THE WELL-KNOWN HOTEL AND BUSINESS PREMISES,
KNOWN AS

The Imperial Hotel, Wexford.

Situate in SELSKAR STREET, WEXFORD, held under Lease for seventy years from 29th September, 1905, at the yearly rent of £54 16s.
DESCRIPTIVE PARTICULARS.

The premises, which are situate in one of the busiest centres of the town of Wexford—at the entrance to the Main Street—within three minutes' walk of the D. and S. E. Railway Station, comprise the well-known HOTEL, including commodious Grocery and Provision Shop, Bar, Public and Private Tap Rooms, Smoke Room, Coffee Room, twelve large Bedrooms, etc , etc

At the rere of the Hotel there is a Large Yard, with entrance from Redmond Place, opposite the Dublin and South Eastern Railway Co.'s Goods Stores. This yard contains very large Stabling Accommodation, large Coach and Motor Houses, Hayshed, Piggery, Bottling Store, Mineral Water Store, Bacon Store and Smoke House, Paper Store, and newly erected Boiler and Wash Houses, etc.

For further particulars and conditions of Sale apply
Messrs. CROTTY AND KELLY, Solicitors, Selskar, Wexford;
Messrs. P. J. O'FLAHERTY AND SON, Solicitors,
Rowe Street, Wexford; or

McCARTHY & CODD,
(n3792-3)   AUCTIONEERS, WEXFORD.

An advertisement announcing the sale of the Imperial Hotel in 1922.

AUCTIONEERS
Kevin Morris, 118 South Main Street
Thomas J. O'Brien, Selskar House, Selskar Street

BAKERS
Godkins, North Main Street
James Kavanagh, 22 North Main Street
Joseph Kelly, 30 Selskar Street

BANKS
Bank of Ireland, The crescent
Munster & Leinster Bank, North Main Street
National Bank, Custom House Quay
Provincial Bank of Ireland, Thomas Ashe Street

CATTLE DEALERS
Fred Doyle Rocklands
James Kirwan, 28 Corish Park

CINEMAS
Abbey, George's Street
Capitol, South Main Street
Wexford Palace Ltd., Harpers Lane

CLEANERS AND DYERS
Imco, 30 South Main Street

CYCLE DEALERS
Seamus Bell, Redmond Place
Alf Cadogan, 67 South Main Street
N. J. Hore 23 South Main Street

DRAPERS
Burton Ltd, North Main Street
W & G Hadden, North Main Street
Healy & Collins, 7 South Main Street
Wm Jenkins, 29 – 33 North Main Street
John P. Rochford, South Main Street
Alex Sloan & Co., 59 Bullring
J. Sullivan, The Bullring

FOOTWEAR
W. Gaynor, 115 North Main Street
Paddy Lyons, South Main Street
E. J. Wheeler, 30 North Main Street
Grocery & Provision Merchants
James Browne, Bishopswater

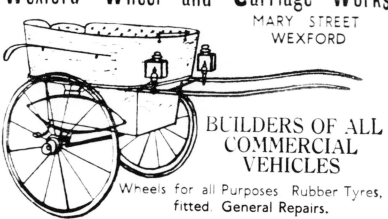
This is a wonderful advertisement for carriages.

This advertisement reminds that cycling to Dublin to watch a match was not unusual.

J. Dillon, Bride Place
Jack Fane, The Bullring
J Ffrench, 27 North Main Street
Foleys General Stores, 106 Selskar Street
William Goodison, Bishopswater
Halligan Bros., Westgate
Home and Colonial Stores, North Main Street
Kelly, Macken Street
Kelly, Barrack Street
L & N Tea Company, 17 South Main Street
Amby Moynihan, King Street
Francis Murphy, Whitemill Road
Peter Murphy, 53 South Main Street
J. H. Stone, 5 South Main Street
Wm. Walker & Son, 78 North Main Street

HAIRDRESSERS
LADIES
Rita Cuddihy, 2 South Main Street
P.J. Doran, Bullring
Eithne, Custom House Quay
La Tulipe, Selskar
Gertrude Moloney, Bullring
O'Mahony's, 111 North Main Street
Ailish Owens, 3 South Main Street
Stella Power, 3 Monck Street
P. Whelan, 6 North Main Street
MEN'S
Byrne, Lower Rowe Street
Carley Brothers South Main street
J. Kelly, 80 South Main Street
John North, King Street
Swords, Monck Street

HARDWARE
W.R. Hamilton, Bullring
McCormack Bros., custom House Quay
P.J. O'Connor, 39-41 North Main Street
S&R Pierce, 32 South Main Street

LAUNDRIES
House of Mercy, St Michael's, Summerhill
Painters & Decorators
Doyle & O'Leary, 17 Distillery Road
Furlong Bros., Westgate
Murphy & Roche, 44 South Main Street
Thomas Power, Clonard

Petrol Distributors
Caltex, Redmond Place
Esso, Redmond Place
Shield Oil Co., Paul Quay.

PUBLICANS
P. Banville, Paul Quay
Des Corish, North Main Street
N Barnwell, 114 South Main Street
Paddy Carey, 83 South Main Street
Cinema Bar, 57 South Main Street
Eagle Bar, 91 North Main Street
Eden Vale Bar, Bullring
Goal Bar, 72 South Main Street
Old White Horse Inn, Commercial Quay
Shamrock Bar, Anne Street
Travers-Purcell, 79 South Main Street
Welcome Inn, Crescent quay

RELIGIOUS GOODS
J. L. Doyle, North Main Street
M. J. Furlong, South Main Street
Mrs. Monaghan, South Main Street

RESTAURANTS & CAFES
Bernie's Café, 90 North Main Street
Forte, 7 North Main Street
Granada Grill, 118 South Main Street
Ita's, 79 North Main Street
Love's Café, 75 North Main Street
Mernagh's, The Bullring
Moran's, Parnell Street
Mrs., O'Toole, South Main Street
Ritz Café, Bullring
Sinnotts, 27 Selskar Street

SHIP OWNERS
Wexford Steamship Co., Paul Quay
Harry Wilson, Commercial Quay

SHOP FITTERS
Crescent Cabinet Co., Church Lane

TAR DISTILLERS
Wexford Gas Consumers Co., Trinity Street

JOHN BARRY

'This is the ship Alliance,
From Philadelphia town;
She proudly bids defiance
to England's king and crown.
As captain of the deck I stand
To guard her banner true;
Half Yankee and half Irishman,
What tyrant's slave are you?'
-From Jack Barry by William Collins

The Scots claim John Paul Jones as 'Founder of the American Navy', but here in Wexford we know that John Barry is the acclaimed 'Father of the American Navy'.

John Barry, sometimes called ' Jack Barry', was born on a smallholding at Ballysampson, Tacumshane, about 10 miles from Wexford. The year was 1745 and Wexford of that era was a growing port. In fact, Barry is said to have first put to sea from Wexford on board a ship skippered by his uncle. In 1759 Barry was 14 years old as he sailed out of Wexford harbour bound for America.

Having crossed the Atlantic, he was to settle in Philadelphia where he found employment as a seaman. Over the next few years, Barry sailed on trading ships plying along the American coast and to the West Indies. In 1766, the 22-year-old Wexfordman became skipper of the schooner, Barbados. Through hard work and good seamanship, Barry then became a shipowner. His first craft was a sloop, later replaced by a bigger ship, *Black Prince.*

With the outbreak of the American Revolutionary War against Britain, Barry presented his ship to Congress. In April of 1776, John Barry provided the rebel forces with one of its greatest morale boosters in a gloomy year. As captain of an ancient brigantine named *Lexington*, the wily Irishman lured the British navy ship, *HMS Edward* to within hailing distance before engaging her in a running battle. This engagement resulted in the surrender of the *Edward*, giving the fledgling American Navy its very first prize.

Late in 1776, Barry took command of the 32-gun *Effingham* but when the British captured Philadelphia he burned her to prevent her falling into enemy hands. However he was to use her boats with muffled oars to harass the British supply ships on the Delaware, using his intimate knowledge of the many creeks and channels. So successful were these raids that General Howe is said to have offered Barry $100,000 and a position in the British Navy if he would cease. John Barry refused to change sides.

Over the next few years, John Barry skippering various craft was involved in attempts to breach the blockade placed on the 'rebel held' coast.

In 1781 he was put in charge of a 36-gun frigate, *Alliance*, one of the finest ships built in America to that time. In this craft he was to capture many valuable prizes for the newly emerging nation. In 1781, after the fall of Yorktown, Barry was assigned to return Lafayette to France. And it was on board the *Alliance* that John Barry fought in the last naval battle of that war on 10 March 1783.

Following the war, he returned to merchant shipping, sailing as far as China. But by 1794, Barry was again a navy man. On 4 June of that year, he was appointed Commander in Chief of all American Naval Forces. As commander of *United States*, the first custom built American warship he took on the task of protecting United States

This is a group photo of the committee involved in the building of the club. Back row Paddy Quirke, Tom McGuinness, Tom Rossiter, Michael Murphy, Humphry Moore, Stan Malone, Har Peare, Michael Terry, Michael Reddy. Front row John Myrtle, Nicky Rossiter, John Hendrick, Father Harry Sinnott, Peter O'Connor and Johnny Byrne. Missing from the photo were Oliver Sinnott, Harry Hogan, M. Dempsey and J Walshe.

shipping. During undeclared hostilities with France, he commanded all American warships in the West Indies and though a combination of seamanship and ignoring foolish orders he preserved his ship and crew. It was John Barry who undertook the task of carrying his countries envoy to France to negotiate the end to the hostilities.

His French connection continued in 1803 when Barry was a signatory of the register at the marriage in Baltimore in 1803 of Elizabeth Patterson to Jerome Bonaparte.

John Barry died on 13 September 1803 at the age of fifty-eight. In September 1956, President Sean T. O'Kelly unveiled a statue at The Crescent in Wexford. The statue had arrived by U.S. naval ship and was a gift from the people of the United States of America to the birthplace of 'The Father of The American Navy.' Today, John Barry Day is celebrated in Wexford when not only this great seaman, but all Wexford seafarers are remembered, particularly those who died at sea.

FATHER SINNOTT'S

The late 1950s and early 1960s were not boom times. The Celtic Tiger was not even a remote idea. People worked hard when they could find work, many had to take the boat to England. Rock and Roll music was coming into it's own. Television was on the horizon and teenagers were being invented. Maybe it was this phenomenon of the alien being, the teenager, that spurred on the priest for the Bride Street parish to think of starting a boys club. Then again it may have been the growth in corporation estates in the general area. Bishopswater was still the new houses at Distillery Road but there were also St Aidan's Crescent, Corish Park and the looming of Kennedy Park along with the older estates. Whatever the reason, this priest – Harry Sinnott - mobilised the people.

Carpenters, painters, welders, brickies, shop assistants and just about any other occupation came together to become builders.

In an era before the spectre of insurance, planning notices and the like this motley crew started digging foundations for a building designed if memory serves me right, by a carpenter. Initially they got it wrong. They dug for weeks but could not get a solid foundation so they moved a couple of hundred feet to the present site. Remember this was before the JCB and foundation trenches like First World War relics were dug with pick, shovel and buckets. They worked in the factories by day, got the tea and were on site within an hour through winter and summer.

I do not have an idea of where the money came from. I have an inkling that Harry Sinnott wheeled and dealt with suppliers and they probably amazed themselves with their subsequent generosity. There was some fund raising with silver circles, nap cards and the like.

The great fundraiser for younger people was the field day. One abiding memory is the magnificent slide constructed in John Conboy's field. There was a fabulous hill facing the tail end houses of Bishopswater – ending in a boggy swamp. On this hill the volunteers (there was little shortage of that commodity in 1962) built a slide about 150 feet long with hardboard base and timber sides. For a few pennies you got a hemp mat and away you went. It wasn't the big dipper but it was ours, cheap and fun. I remember at one time Father Sinnott got hold of an 8mm or 16mm projector and showed the film of the Von Trapp Family – not the musical The Sound of Music, it has not appeared.

The official opening featured 'Merry Moments' presented by St Bridget's Concert Group. There were songs by Nancy Doyle, soprano and step dancing from P. Kehoe and P. O'Reilly. Eddie Hopkins's Showband gave us 'Pick of the Pops'. There was a selection of Irish Airs from The Slaneyside Ceili Band and songs from tenor, Seamus Cullen. Sean Rattigan performed a violin solo after a dramatized version of 'Kevin Barry'. The Hopkins Sister danced, as did the Gaul School of Irish Dancing and St Bridgid's Trio. After 18 separate items the evening ended with a one-act operetta called The Elopement. The programme was presented on Sunday and Monday 14 and Tuesday 15 October 1962 to accommodate the large audience.

There were also concerts and of course pongo, not bingo. Pongo made great use of the bottle tops to mark the numbers on wooden boards rather than printed cards. These were obtained from Jimmy Browne's pub. There was no talk of recycling but whereas now the bingo halls use up forests of trees tin those days you changed the board for every few games – no waste.

Basketball was the great new sport introduced by the club. GAA was important and was a mainstay but this import was great. There were players from all over town. I also recall a big steel bar for gymnastics. It was up on the stage and was very popular. My abiding memory is jumping from a form (our word for the long wooden bench an pronounced furm) to this bar, hands sliding off and slapping onto the stage.

Cross-country running was another sport introduced to us by St Joseph's. I remember the late Toddy and Tom Rossiter being involved in that. Father Sinnott used to load full teams into his car to go to the events around the country.

Table tennis and handball were also catered for along with football and hurling.

I won't even try to name the committee members and helpers because I have no wish to offend any of these great people by missing one out. What I do recall about them was that although most had children using the facilities there were a number who had no such family benefit but still gave of their time and energy. In many ways they were the unpaid and unpraised social workers, youth leaders and community activists of their day.

Among the tradesmen who gave their services free of charge to St Josephs were Frankie Hore, Willie Edwards, Toddy Rossiter, Oliver Sinnott, Paddy Quirke, John Hendrick, Padge Kelly, John Reck and Bennie Underwood. (Rossiter Collection)

To the members of the club I can only remind you with items that will mean nothing to the general readers. Remember Humphry and Har? Did you build dams?

SOME OLD WEXFORD SHOPS

George Bridges kept Wexford informed of the countdown to Christmas, much as the millennium people did. From mid summer his adverts announced the number of weeks left. We all knew that the festive season was really here when George opened his extra showroom down Trimmers Lane. In the pre-supermarket and toy catalogue days this was the Aladdin's Cave where the wish lists finally took shape.

Walkers Mall was once a single shop called Walkers. The abiding memory is of freshly ground coffee long before many of us ever tried that exotic brew. That smell wafted out into the street.

Rainbow Valley Boutique was a true child of the flower power generation. I recall that it was started by a group of young people – who I recall but will not name - yet. It was upstairs in a building in Oyster Lane. In some ways the location was a minus as a number of girls are said to have been reluctant to go into a shop run by young lads.

Jack Fanes was a traditional pub cum grocery shop with a little snug inside the door for the ladies before the days of equal pub rights. It also had an interesting elevator to the cellar, which was located just inside the door. It was a shop that was very popular with country people and those interested in GAA and horses. A regular patron there was Jackie Culleton a very well known dentist who had his practice nearby.

Coffeys was immortalized in a tune by the 'boys band' or to give them their proper title St Patrick's Fife and Drum Band. To many Wexford people Coffeys was immortalized in the famous 'approbation system'. This was a method of selling clothes and other goods when some people were either too busy or too shy to visit the shop. Getting a new jacket or pair of shoes meant that someone, usually the wife and mother, visited the shop a pick a number of possibilities. The messenger boy on

This one of the many teams associated with the club – football, hurling, handball, table tennis, basketball and cross-country were included. (Rossiter Collection)

his distinctive bike with advertising plate and huge basket holder then delivered these to the home. The desired item was chosen in the comfort and privacy of the house – with everyone contributing a comment and the rest were returned. The majority of the items were then paid for 'on the book' by weekly payments. There would be queues of people paying accounts on Saturday mornings. We only ever realized that approbation was a word when the sales were on and big signs went up – no approbation or credit during the sale.

Woolworth's came and went in Wexford in less than fifty years. When it was there it was magical. It was a shop with origins in the magical USA. It introduced the idea of limited self-service in many sections – there was always the assistant behind that wide counter. The big thrill was the wide varieties of goods on offer under one roof and the amount of gadgets and novelties. Soft whipped ice cream cornets – we did not get cones – were a great attraction just inside the door. It was there that most of us encountered a 99 when a flake was inserted or having a choice of 'hundreds and thousands' or strawberry syrup on the cornet.

Sinnott's the Chemists was one of many small family chemists in Wexford. People held all chemists in those days in certain awe. Mr. Sinnott was a prime example of this. He was well known for concocting his own remedies for many ailments. One that I recall was a cough medicine that had the magical name of hippo wine squills and glycerin. He was later semi legendary for a lotion that cured aromatic feet.

TVRS was not the first record shop in Wexford but it was a very important step into modern times. They were probably the first shop dedicated solely to music and carrying a wide range of records. The main claim to fame was the introduction of the listening station where you could listen in private to a record before purchasing. In the past if you wanted to hear a song you had to ask to have it played over the shop system.

Chip Shops were an institution before the days of big Macs and flame grilled whoppers.

I will never recall them all but here goes. Nellie Wrights was one of our favourites because it was near to Roche's Terrace our family outpost. Nellie and Gordon who worked in the shop at the end of Bride Street were conspicuous by their English accents as much as for the lovely chips. Kevin Roche's was on South Main Street and was a popular venue for eating after a night out in the Cinema Palace. It was a lovely place to sit in at the long tables and eat from enamel plates and hear the film critics in full flow. Peter Dempsey's at Parnell Street provided a similar service for Capitol Cinema. His specialty was pig's feet and mushy peas. Of course the patrons of The Abbey also had a chipper. For them it was Stamps in John Street. My main recollection of that establishment was that we went there for our lunch when attending George's Street School.

Myths and Legends of Maudlintown and The Faythe

This part of Wexford is named after the parish of St Mary Magdalene or Maud, to whom a church and a leper hospital were dedicated here circa 1176. In the main these lepers were not afflicted like those in the Bible but were people suffering skin disorders due to the diet of the time. The hospital was probably on the site of the present graveyard, which is relatively new. A holy well dedicated to Mary Magdalene was covered over in 1935. The pattern was held on 22 July each year until then. The name of Mary Magdalene continues in the houses of Magdalene's Terrace built on the site of a brewery, of 1840. Within the housing complex of Maudlintown are various avenues, recalling the seafaring past of Wexford.

Hantoon Road and Antelope Road recall ships built in and sailed in from Wexford. A lane, leads to 'the Rocks' with beautiful open fields and large rock outcrops. Pr or to quarrying one of these larger outcrops, called Trespan, was reputedly the location for Cromwell's guns as they battered the Castle of Wexford in October 1649. The steep rise in the fields here is known as Cronock's Bower It was a popular venue for sledges usually plastic sacks after snowfalls. The Bower is also reputed to be the site of midnight revels at midsummer in older times. On those nights a huge bonfire blazed and the ounger people from all parts of the town gathered to dance round it. The story goes that the Redemptorist Mission Fathers at the newly built Twin Churches condemned the practice in 1858.

In 1540 there was FFAYGHTT STRETE recorded in Wexford. The name Faythe is traced to 'Faiche' an Irish word translated as a green or fair green A fair was held here on the 24 August each year. In the 1700s it was referred to as a poor area with no schools. In 1860 it was said to consist of snug cabins, housing some of the most industrious people on earth, who were mainly employed in weaving nets and spinning hemp. Into the twentieth century many men from this are remained in maritime trades including lighthouse or lightship duty. A common sight was the wagon collecting their provisions in special waterproof wicker baskets.

Faythe Harriers club is highly respected and is involved in Hurling, Football and Camogie. The club originated as the Mulgannon Harriers and was a major social club, with the ever-popular billiards and card games. Bernadette Place was built n 1957. Almost opposite Bernadette P ace entrance is the St John of God Primary School. This school was built on the site of the first Christian Brothers School, opened in Wexford in 1849. Under the St John of God Nuns it became an infant and fema e school in 1875. Wexford fishermen erected the statue of Our Lady, Star of the Sea at the school in 1954.

Carnivals were held in a field opposite the school in the 1950s. Just a few houses

Swan View in the early 1900s (Lawrence Collection)

north of the school, in 1840, a ropewalk was established, which reached down to William Street. Another ropewalk was situated almost directly opposite, stretching to the area known as "the Rocks".

Swan View was probably the site of the Fa r. The swan, which gives the area its title, is one of metal. Robert Stafford, a merchant, who was Mayor of Wexford, erected the fountain in 1851 The trees here are relatively new; previously there was just a wide-open square. This open area was a popular place for meetings and rallies. Most of the public meetings of the 1911 Lockout were held here. In 1941 De Valera reviewed a large gathering of military volunteers, nurses and Local Defence Forces at Swan View. It was in the Faythe area that Huguenot refugees settled in the early 1700s.

John Boyle O'Reilly recalls the Faythe in the ballad, *The Faythe Fishing Craft*. It commemorates a tragedy on St Martin's Eve, when 65 women of the Faythe are reputed to have been made widows by the tragic drown ng of the r husbands in Wexford Bay. The date of this tragedy varies between 10 and 12 November and the years 1833 and 1762. Whether it is fact or fable, few agree. The trad t on against putting to sea on St Martin's Eve was usually observed, but on that day the tempting sight of an easy catch lured the fishermen out. Tradition states that St Martin mounted on a wh te steed was seen po nting to the shore on the fateful day. For many years after no Wexford fisherman challenged the belief of St Martin's Eve.

THE STREETS OF WEXFORD

This listing of Wexford Street and the origins of the names is restricted to the older sections of a rapidly expanding town. Many of the more recent titles for streets and estates are descriptive or related to the former owners of the land.

ABBEY – takes its name from Selskar Abbey. It was called Lower Back Street in 1649.

ALLEN - is named after the Rev. Joseph Allen who owned a large portion of the land. It was opened as a street by Robert Allen and later paved by the Corporation in 1793. It was known as BROAD Street in the 1600s.

ALVINA BROOK - built by Pierce's Foundry in the 1940s, the name is a sort of hybrid with Brook referring to the river running at the rear of the houses and Alvina a possible corruption of the Gaelic alainn or beautiful.

ANNE - probably named after a Queen Anne. It was earlier known as THE FLESH MARKET and THE SHAMBLES when butchers carried on trade here in the early 1800s. The official name Thomas Ashe Street

ARD CARMAN - is a Gaelic translation of a descriptive location i.e. Wexford Heights.

ASHFIELD DRIVE - in the 1980s the naming of estates and streets became overrun with titles denoting possible features of the earlier times, hence Ash Field Drive.

ASHLEIGH PARK - another descriptive title.

AVENUE de FLANDRES - built by Pierce and Company and named after the location of their Paris office in Rue de Flandres.

AVONDALE DRIVE - named after Charles Stewart Parnell's estate in Wicklow, Avondale.

BARRACK - named after the Military Barracks located here on the site of the old Wexford Castle.

BATT'S - takes its name from Jane Batt owner of a large part of the land.

BAYVIEW DRIVE - from its location overlooking Wexford Bay.

BEECHLAWN - is most likely from a fanciful lawn surrounded by beech trees.

BELVEDERE GROVE - takes the name from Belvedere House, which overlooked the area. Wexford Male Voice Choir and Wexford Historical Society founder Dr. George Hadden lived in the house.

BERNADETTE PLACE - after Street Bernadette of Lourdes fame.

BISHOP'S PARK - named for its proximity to Bishopswater.

BISHOPSWATER - takes its name from the stream running down behind Alvina Brook. Locally it is called The Horse River, but it is said to flow from a well blessed by a Bishop of Ferns in times past.

BRENDAN CORISH GARDENS – named after Brendan Corish T.D. and Tanaiste and son of Richard Corish.

BRIDE - taken from the Gaelic Brid for Bridget the name of the parish and an ancient church in the area.

BULLRING - named after the sport of bull baiting carried on here in the 1600s. It has been known as The Common Plain and Fountain Square.

CARRICK LAWN - takes its name from the townland, which in turn is named after the lawn or meadow of Carrick.

CARRIGEEN - is named from the Gaelic for Little Rock, after a stone outcrop on which it is built.

CASA RIO - built by Pierce and Company, the name comes from the Latin for 'House on the River'.

CASEMENT TERRACE - commemorates Sir Roger Casement, it was named at the time his body was being returned to Ireland.

CASTLE HILL - was the hill beside the old Wexford Castle.

CHARLOTTE - this name dating from the early 1800s probably recalls a queen or princess.

CINEMA LANE - was named by locals when Wexford's first cinema, The Palace, opened here in 1914. The official name is Harpur's Lane.

CLIFFORD - named after James Clifford the landowner. It was once called The Deddery.

CLONARD AVENUE - named after the parish/townland. Literally translated as 'high meadow'.

COMMERCIAL QUAY - describes the earlier use of this quay for commercial as opposed to government or customs use.

COMMON QUAY - leads from COMMON QUAY which would have been a sort of 'free quay' when most of the other sections were privately owned. May be similar to common land on mountains etc.

COOLCOTTS LANE - this name has at least two interpretations from the Gaelic. *Coill na Coitte* or the 'wood of the cotts' denoting a wood where timber to construct the boats called cotts was grown. *Cul Cotts*, the back of Kaat's meaning behind Van Kaat's shipyard at Westgate.

CORISH PARK - is named after Richard Corish who was mayor of Wexford for 25 consecutive years until his death in 1945.

CORNMARKET - was the official Norman site designated for the sale of corn.

CORRY'S VILLAS - recalls businessman and athlete Jim Corry who donated the land to Wexford Corporation for housing.

CRESENT QUAY - named for the curved quay, called The Elliptic Quay during construction in the mid 1800s.

CROKE AVENUE - named after Archbishop Croke (1824-1902) GAA and Gaelic League supporter. Croke Park in Dublin is also named after him.

CUSTOM HOUSE QUAY - named as the site of one of the many customhouses that featured in the busy port's history.

DAVITT RD. - from Michael Davitt founder of the Land League.

DEVEREUX VILLAS - named after Richard Devereux, businessman, ship owner and philanthropist of the 19th century. The pronunciation is DEV-ER-EX not like gateaux.

DISTILLERY RD. - takes the name from Bishopswater Distillery that was founded in 1827.

DONOVAN'S WHARF – beside the Crescent and presumably named after a former businessman.

FARNOGUE - takes its name from the river Farnogue that entered the Slaney at this point.

FAYTHE - from Faiche or Faigh meaning an open space or plain. The name Ffayghtt was used on a map in 1540.

FERNDALE PARK - another description denoting a dale filled with ferns.

FISHER'S ROW – taken from the occupation of a large number of the residents a century ago.

FRANCIS Street - from Saint Francis whose order of friars founded a church near here in 1240. It was previously called James Street.

GEORGE'S - possibly from the king's name.

GLENA TERRACE. - Most likely derived from Glen.

GREEN – named after John Green (e), seven times mayor of Wexford.

GROGAN'S ROAD – named from the Grogan family, later Knox-Grogan of Johnstown Castle. It was colloquially called Bishop's Street in 1636 and Hospital Road in the mid 1800s.

HARRIS'S LANE - from the family owning the land.

HENRIETTA – is another royal title.

HIGH – was a common name for a main thoroughfare in medieval times.

HILL – is descriptive of the terrain.

IVY LANE - descriptive.

JOHN'S DRIVE/ROAD/AVENUE – derived from Saint John, title of the parish and church. John's Street was the first, the as streets were opened, road, drive, avenue etc. were named. All of these streets should have Saint as a prefix.

JOHN'S GATE - one of the medieval gates of Wexford, John's Gate, was located here.

JOSEPH - named after Saint Joseph's School opened here by the Christian Brothers.

KAAT'S LANE - led to the shipyard of Van Kaat in the mid 1600s.

KENNEDY PARK - after President John Fitzgerald Kennedy of the United States of America.

KEYSAR'S LANE - is a Norse name meaning "Lane of the Ship Wharf", it is one of the oldest recorded thoroughfares in Wexford.

KING'S – was a common generic name in most towns.

LAMBERT PLACE - origin undetermined but probably from landowners.

LIAM MELLOWE'S PARK - named after an Irish patriot.

MALLIN - from a 1916 leader. More common name is Back Street.

MANNIX PLACE - named after Bishop Mannix.

MANSFIELD DRIVE - descriptive, possibly inspired by Austen's Mansfield Park.

MARY - after Saint Mary or the Virgin Mary, it comes from the original parish and church.

MAUDLINTOWN - a corruption of Street Mary Magdalene and the parish and leper hospital of medieval times.

McCLURE MEADOWS – is named for Robert McClure one of the crew that discovered the Northwest Passage. He was born in Wexford.

MEADOWVALE – is descriptive, meadow in a vale.

MENAPIA AVENUE – is from the old Celtic name of Wexford on a map dated AD 150, Menapia.

MICHAEL – is from Saint Michael the Archangel and the original medieval parish and church.

MILL ROAD - a flourmill owned by Devereux was located here reputed to be one of the largest in Ireland.

MONCK - after George Monck, Duke of Albemarle who was granted the ferry and lands in 1658.

MULGANNON - probably derived from Mullagh meaning a summit and gamhan meaning a calf i.e. The Hill of the Calf.

NEWLANDS - descriptive

NEWLINE RD. - a new road built as part of Famine Relief work.

NEWTOWN COURT/ROAD - based on the name of the general area.

OAK TREE RISE - descriptive

O'CONNELL AVENUE - after Daniel O'Connell.

O'RAHILLY PLACE - after a historical figure.

OYSTER LANE – is from the consumption of oysters in the taverns that lined the street.

PARK - part of the ancient town parklands of Wexford where the gentry could hunt.

PARKLANDS - from the lands of the ancient park

PARKSIDE - as above

PARNELL – named after Charles Stewart Parnell.

PATRICK'S LANE – is from the medieval parish and church of Street Patrick.

PAUL QUAY - from Pale meaning fortress, Wexford Castle overlooked this quay.

PETER – is from Saint Peter's medieval parish and church.

PINERIDGE – is descriptive, ridge of the pine trees.

PINEWOOD ESTATE – is descriptive, wood of pine trees.

REDMOND PLACE - after the Redmond Family, politicians and businessmen. The area stands on lands reclaimed from the river by the Redmonds.

RICHMOND/RICHMOND TCE - from Richmond House, now the Loreto Convent built by the Duke of Richmond in 1792.

RIVERVIEW TERRACE – is from Riverview House and descriptive of the location with a view of the Slaney.

ROCHE'S ROAD – is named after Father James Roche responsible for building of the twin churches in the 1850s.

ROWE - built by the Rowe family.

SCHOOL - from the Wexford Poor School located here.

SELSKAR – is from the Abbey of Saint Selskar.

SKEFFINGTON – is from participant of 1916 Rising.

SLANEY – is from the river Slaney that lapped here prior to the 1800s land reclamation.

SLANEYVIEW COURT - descriptive

SPAFIELD AVE - built on a field, which had a spa well.

SPAWELL RD. - is descriptive, location of a spa well.

ST AIDAN'S CRESCENT – named after patron saint of diocese.

ST BRENDAN'S RD – named after Street Brendan the Navigator.

ST JOHN'S - see JOHN'S

ST PETER'S - see PETER'S

SUMMERHILL – was commonly a name given to hills, which were only usable in fine or summer weather.

SWANVIEW - from view of fountain shaped as a swan erected here by Mayor Robert Stafford in 1851.

SYCAMORE CLOSE - descriptive

TALBOT GREEN - named by the residents combining the names of Talbot Street and Green Street on which sites the estate was built.

TALBOT - built on land owned by James Talbot.

TEMPERANCE ROW - named after a Temperance Hall built here in the 1800s. This was called Le Cowstrette on a map dated 1540. The area was called Hey Bey on a 19th century map.

THOMAS CLARKE PLACE - from an Irish patriot.

THOMAS - unknown

THE GROVE – is descriptive.

TIVOLI TERRACE - probably derived from continental Tivoli Gardens.

TREES AVE – is descriptive.

TRIMMER'S LANE – is from the occupation of trimming or spreading ballast in the old sailing ships.

TRINITY Street - from an ancient parish of the Holy Trinity.

TUSKAR VIEW – is descriptive of view of Tuskar Rock Light.

WALNUT GROVE - descriptive

WATERLOO RD - named after the Battle of Waterloo. Prior to 1815 it was METHODIST ROW.

WELL LANE – is from location of a well.

WELLINGTON PLACE - after the Duke of Wellington.

WESTGATE - one of the medieval gates into Wexford built circa 1300.

WHITEROCK VIEW - descriptive

WILLIAM Street - possibly from King William

WINDMILLS HILL - from the number of windmills once located here.

WOLF TONE VILLAS - named after Theobald Wolf Tone.

WYGRAM PLACE - built on the lands of Sir Robert Fitzwigram.

On various dates after 1920 the Borough Council agreed to adopt new names for nineteen streets. The changes were:

Charlotte - Colbert

Gibson – Peter

George – Oliver Plunkett

King – Partridge

William – James Connolly★

Wellington Place – O'Rahilly Place

Ram – Skeffington

Monck – McDonagh★

Barrack – Macken★

Talbot – Pearse★

Henrietta – O'Hanrahan★

Hill – Sean McDermott

Back – Mallin

Duke – Thomas Clarke

Waterloo Road – McCurtain Road★

Anne – Thomas Ashe

Common Quay – O'Hanlon Walsh★

Castle Hill – Kevin Barry

High – McSweeney

In a plebiscite in 1932 to legalise the changes only four could be changed – Castle Hill, Back, Ram and Gibson. Others were officially changed later. In true Wexford fashion regardless of changes the general public retained the use of the old names or even invented new ones. The street suggestions marked ★ never seemed to catch on.

THE NEW LANE OR BATT STREET

Before the Second World War or The Emergency this lane on the southern outskirts of Wexford leading to the sea, the railway tracks and the cott safe boasted a wide range of industries. There was a mineral factory, a forge, Keane's chipper, Doran's who made statues and a number of stables. In one of the stables, some locals put on plays including *Murder in the Red Barn* where the smell of donkey droppings surely added authenticity to the production. Access to the cott safe and Browne's Bank was restricted to those owning boats and a watchman was in place to uphold the regulations.

BALLAST BANK

In the original 'Act for the improvement of the town and harbour of Wexford and building a bridge or bridges over the River Slaney at said town' the importance of ballast was evident from the terms laid down. This act was presented to Parliament in the reign of George III, in the early 1790s and the bridge referred to was the oak bridge on which the 1798 executions occurred. It also referred to the plan to construct 'a quay from St Paul's Quay to the Ferry Boat Quay' This was the plan to build the modern quayfront as opposed to the many wharves of earlier times, much of which was completed by the time the famous painting of Wexford in about 1820 was finished.

The corporation – the group of people proposing the act – was to meet at The Courthouse on or before 24 June 1794 to appoint a place to be called the Ballast Office and that it was to be called by that name henceforth. The corporation were charged with furnishing or causing to be furnished ballast to master of ships or vessels. They were also to provide sufficient lighters and gabbards, workmen, tools and engines for raising ballast in such part or parts of the harbour or river as is judged expedient. Ballast was to be made available within 24 hours of notice being given to the Ballast Master. If wind and weather prevented this, it was to be completed within 12 hours of the weather permitting. One or more wharves were to be erected for saving and storing ballast. The Ballast Master had power to direct ships to the Ballast Wharf, which relieved the corporation of providing lighters and gabbards to load ballast. There was a charge of 7 pence per ton for ballast loaded and the Ballast Master paid 2 pence per ton for ballast unloaded. Any ship's master taking ballast from anywhere other than the Ballast Wharf was liable to fine of up to £10 to be paid to the person informing the corporation. The Customs Officers did not allow ships to clear customs, unless they had a receipt from the Ballast Master. The present Ballast Bank was erected in 1831 and was probably agreed on as it meant increasing the working area of the quay with no ballast storage needed.

When a ship needed ballast, it made its way to the man-made island of The Ballast Bank in the harbour and followed this procedure. A small boat was lowered and 2 men rowed over to the Ballast Bank with a rope from the ship's bow. This rope was made fast to the bank and the men rowed back to the ship. The rope was connected to the hand-winch and with this, the men hove the ship into the bank. The ballast man would then load about 20 tons of sand aboard. This was placed or trimmed so that the boat was balanced. The rope was then loosed and the ship could sail.

In 1850 Edward Murphy and Patrick Dempsey, contractors, were paid £10 for repairs to Ballast Bank 15 May. In October 1857 John Maddock, Windmill Hills, was awarded a one-year contract to supply ballast gravel on board ships at 10d per ton. A surety of £100 was requested from him. In 1909 Captain Brady reported that there was room for 500 to 600 tons of ballast on the Ballast Bank. The Harbour Commissioners decided to buy it at 1 penny a ton if it was good quality.

In 1945 there were reports that a person was interested in purchasing the Ballast Bank. In 1947 the County Council complained that the Ballast Bank was damaged and in danger of falling on the north side. The Harbour Commissioners reported that they did not have the money for repairs. In 1973 ABS donated a pump to Corporation in November for possible use on the Ballast Bank. This referred to a plan to erect a fountain on the Ballast Bank. The front-page story in a local newspaper of 1973 had a headline that read 'Fountains Scheme for Ballast Bank'. The story stated that the large fountain pump donated by ABS Pumps could possibly be used by a Junior Chamber project involving the Ballast Bank. It appears that the Junior Chamber had decided to drop the festival lighting venture and were looking for a new idea. The idea of a permanent illuminated fountain was put forward by Danny Keating and generally adopted. Maurice Moore, chapter president felt that it would be an ideal way to illuminate the harbour. He paid tribute to ABS for the spontaneous gesture and said that the company might provide assistance in bringing power to the Ballast Bank. Mayor Des Corish who had received the fountain on behalf of Wexford stated that the corporation would consider the matter. Here the story ended.

Murder in Cinema Lane

On Saturday 8 March 1958 at around 11 pm a man was beaten unconscious, with injuries that proved fatal, in his little sweet shop which was a few steps from a popular local cinema – The Palace – and just yards from the busy South Main Street junction with pubs and chippers. The sweet shop, The Dainty, was very popular with those going to 'the pictures' at the Cinema Palace and the street itself though a lane without footpaths was well used as it connects the quays to the main street. Yet on that tragic night no one appears to have seen the killers. The victim, Mr. Hannan was used to keeping the shop open late and even had a small area in the rear where he indulged in his hobby of printing during the intervals between customers. One of his most popular publications was *St Columcille's Prophecies.*

Gardai believe that the killers entered the shop as customers before attacking Mr. Hannan. When they fled, co-incidence helped them avoid being noticed. Just a short time earlier, a car had driven into the water at The Crescent and a large crowd of onlookers would have paid little attention to the fleeing killers. Despite intensive inquiries, the murder in 'The Dainty' remains unsolved.

Bird Shows

One very popular pastime in the mid-twentieth century was the rearing and showing of cage birds. These ranged from canaries to budgies and linnets to more exotic imported varieties. Almost every street had a bird fancier with the shed built out the back.

These were a very different species to the pigeon fanciers who also dotted the urban landscape and could be identified by either the flocks of pigeons circling the area or by being spotted in the early morning heading off with the large wicker basket on the carrier of the bicycle.

The other bird fanciers also dealt in boxes – especially at show time. Shows were held all over the country and Wexford enthusiasts were to be seen heading for the railway station with big black crates. Inside these were show cages all neatly designed to fit snugly into the space available. Show cages were works of art in themselves. I cannot recall if different styles were used for different species but I do remember the ones for canaries. They were painted black on the outside and a sky blue colour on the interior. Many of the birdmen constructed these cages themselves.

Wexford was also a venue for these bird shows and two of the buildings that I recall were the Loch Garman Bandroom in High Street and the St Iberius Hall in

Common Quay Street – now the ESB shop. In later years shows have been held in the Vocational School. The shows were major logistical undertakings. Crates of birds had to be collected from the station, night watchmen had to be appointed from the committee to look after these precious charges. The cages had to arranged, category stickers attached and a catalogue produced.

Rearing these show birds was almost a full time task and required a rudimentary knowledge of biology, nutrition and husbandry. Many of the fanciers bred their own birds and even crossbred to produce winners. I remember some canaries had a special food to bring out a redder hue to the generally accepted yellow plumage. Breeding the birds was like a lottery. There was the anticipation of the egg laying. Then there was the worry about incubation. Thunder was a major problem with many birds being lost if a thunderstorm erupted at a crucial stage. Many a father and son or daughter could be seen walking head down on areas like the Rocks Road – now Mulgannon – after Sunday Mass. They were not looking for lost coins but picking dandelions to feed to the birds.

Hardware stores and many small shops also stocked birdseed, millet and other requirements. As a spin off to the shows many other people had canaries and budgies as pets. These powered an industry for little ladders, mirrors, bells, cuttle fish and a rake of other treats for the Joeys and Pollys.

The judges were usually from outside the area and after long deliberations rosettes, plaques and cups were awarded with the presentation taking place usually on the Sunday afternoon. Bird shows still take place and there are still fanciers and enthusiasts but it does not seem to have the community wide appeal of that golden age.

MONEY

Today everyone has a bank account or a credit union or building society account, often whether they want one or not. Fifty years ago things were very different. The banks were only for those with plenty of money and the vast majority never stepped inside their doors. But they had their own systems of credit and saving, some imported from abroad and others of unknown origin.

One of these, which I have not been able to trace to a source, is The Club. These were usually organised by housewives among friends and acquaintances. The method was that a number of people – again mainly women – signed up for the club. They agreed a weekly sum that they would pay for each 'number or turn'. In the late 1950s this was five shillings in at least one club.

When the list was ready, a calendar was taken out and the names written on slips of paper were drawn and written beside the date – usually a Saturday – this was that persons 'turn'. Every week the subscription was collected and something like 95% of the income was handed over to the member whose turn it was on that week. One of the incentives for this form of saving was that from all the names, one was drawn in a lottery and they received a free 'turn'. The clubs were very popular ways of saving and many people opted for two, three or even four 'turns' in a cycle. The cycle of any club depended on the number of members. There was a lesson in social interaction in the clubs as people often negotiated between them to change the dates of the 'turns' to coincide with family expenses.

Another interesting aspect of the club was the sense of community and trust that they fostered. Here was a housewife, probably without great education or financial skills and she was trusted with hard earned cash and allowed to draw lots to see when anyone was to get a return. There was also the social interaction in collecting and distributing the money. This was often a job given to sons or daughters who learned the need for safety and security and often reaped a nice tip when they delivered the few pounds of the 'turn'.

An imported financial institution very popular in Wexford was the Tontine Society. The idea was brought from France by Philip Pierce whose company had an office in Paris, to help the workers in his factory, which was one of our biggest employers. The Tontine Society was elegant in its simplicity and purpose. At a time when workers live mainly a hand to mouth existence there was little chance of saving either for special occasions or emergencies. In the late 1800s Christmas was becoming more of a commercial than a religious holiday and people needed to have that extra few bob so the Tontine grew.

The Tontine operated in a similar manner to the clubs. Members paid an agreed weekly sum throughout the year. At Christmas or a few weeks before, a payout was made. This was comprised of most of the money lodged with a small sum going to the organizer. This person also made some money in interest on money lodged during the year. Their expenses included bookkeeping, printing of cards and the hours spent collecting.

But that was not all. The Tontine Society was established originally to help people pay that one inevitable expense in life – the funeral. With the urbanization of society and poor laws and pauper's graves, a proper funeral was very high in peoples list of priorities. The Tontine Society helped with this in a rather ingenious and socially responsible way. On the death of a member, the society was informed and a 'death' was marked in the books. This meant that each member paid an extra few pence on top of their weekly subscription and this sum multiplied by the number of members was paid to the family of the deceased. Tontine Societies became very popular in Wexford and sprang up in almost every district of the town. I remember two that my family was paying into because I usually accompanied my father when paying these and later I was deputized to bring the money down. One was operated by Roche's in King Street – Joe was a barber so very often people combined a haircut or shave with paying the society. They usually collected on a Saturday evening.

The main one that I recall was in the Faythe in a little thatched house. They were open on Sunday morning after mass up to dinnertime – we didn't do lunch then. I remember the heart sinking as we rounded The Swan to see a queue of 20 or 30 people waiting to pay. You lined up along the hall, entered in turn into the parlor. There, two or three people sat at a table covered in a heavy cloth and noted your subscription in a ledger and on your payment card. The queuing was murder for the youngsters but it provided another social contact for the adults as news was circulated.

A later financial institution was the Thrift Fund or Penny Bank. It was and in some cases still is a way to save outside the major money markets. These were savings schemes often based in geographic areas whereby specific sums were saved each week with a payout for Christmas. In many cases these were operated to help raise funds for clubs and organizations. The saver did not get interest but rather paid a percentage for the benefit of using the system and this combined with interest accrued on the weekly lodgments kept many organizations afloat from boys clubs to parish halls.

The pawnshop or pawn office as we often called them in Wexford was another financial aspect of life. Item such as clothes, pieces of jewellery or even furniture were put into the shop on Monday in return for a sum of money. These were then redeemed on payday, often to repeat the process again. There is a joke that many men had indigo serge suits. When asked what the indigo was people were told in the go on Monday and out on Friday. The best known pawnshop in Wexford in the mid 1900s was owned by Coffey's and located in George's Street but was always referred to as 'Davy Tobin's' after the man who managed it.

Another often-used financial service in those days was the loan from the family grocer. These shopkeepers, usually located in every street in town, would operate a credit system for groceries with bills being paid off on payday. In many instances they would loan cash if people were in need and this was added to the 'book'.

SCHOOL
THE PRES

Ah the best days of your life or not. In the 1950s we all started off with the nuns. For me it was the Presentation. Regardless of where you lived, most likely you were sent to the convent school that your mother had attended.

The school and schoolyard of my days in the Pres are now buried under apartments opposite Dr Curtis' surgery. They were hidden behind a high thick wall and access was through a gate about 7 feet high by 5 feet wide – no car access was needed in those days.

Stepping through that gate on Waterloo Road you were confronted with a long yard stretching down to a field. If my memory is right there was a field visible to the right as well. Also if my memory is not playing tricks these fields were working farms to the extent that cattle were kept on them. Those were days before playing fields for schools were considered essential.

The boys classes – babies, senior infants and first class were along on the left. The girls' classes all the way up to sixth were in the remaining area. I cannot recall the 'nun' name of my first teacher in the Pres but I believe that she was a local girl of the Curran family. She was young and nice, or so my memory tells me. In that classroom we were introduced to education. The first instruments were slate boards and chalk. I think the classroom had two doors – one from the front yard and another exiting onto the enclosed yard at the other side. There was strict segregation of the boys and girls at playtime in two yards.

I think there was another internal door that led to a few steps down into another room. In that room we found a huge rocking horse and an ancient nun. Well she was ancient to us. That was Sister Bridget the champion of the 'black babies'. This was our introduction to a world and a population outside our Wexford. She told us of these poor suffering mites and encouraged donations of all the pennies we could find. That reminds me of another fund raising idea from those days. As far as I can recall there was a card with a picture of a rosary beads and for each donation you pricked a bead.

As we increased in knowledge and age we went into senior infants – a very different kettle of fish. Here we started the hard grind under the watchful eye of Sister Ibar.

I cannot recall too much of the physical side of those first two classes, probably because I was too young. First Class with Sister Anthony was different. I recall her as of low stature and prominent teeth and that huge rosary beads clicking as she walked around. The pupils sat in long desks – about six or seven feet wide with inkwells, brass covers and a slot underneath for the copies and books. Remember those writing copies with red and blue lines and the sums (not maths yet) copies with the squares?

I recall that there were a number of desks facing toward the top of the room and one along under the window. There must have been a number of pupils at that desk but I can only picture one. He was Peter Stafford of the Cromwell's Fort Staffords. The story at the time we moved on to the CBS was that he continued to study in the Pres but on reflection it is more likely that he went to boarding school. We had no inkling of such things and assumed that either he moved with us or stayed with the nuns.

In the Pres I remember that some people brought their lunches and others got their lunches. The latter we saw got big jam buns but I am sure they got other food as well. Because my cousin Pat (Patricia) Jordan (God rest her) was exactly 50 weeks older than me and lived closer to the school, as I got older she brought me to her house on Roche's Terrace for dinner some days. There Aunt Peggy dished up lovely chips. We ended our sojourn in the Pres with the making of the First Holy Communion. Today this happens in the local parish churches but back then it was sort of 'in house'. The girls in the white dresses and veils and the boys in ill-fitting suits with short trousers trooped into the nuns' chapel of the convent for the ceremony with the mammies and daddies in attendance.

THE PRIMARY

After the First Holy Communion we were transferred to The Brothers or the CBS at Green Street or Thomas Street. Being all of eight years old we were now well into travelling alone to school and from Bishopswater this meant 'up the bank'. We set off down the street, climbed the wall into the Knock and then up the well-worn 'bank' into St Aidan's Crescent. From there we went via Devereux Villas onto Green Street and down to the school. The bank was worn down more than a few feet from the original by all those feet that preceded us. In the summer it was pretty easy although it got slippery with dust as those always-sunny days of our young summers stretched out. Then there were the wet days and how life changed. The trail 'up the bank' could resemble a torrent from an Indiana Jones film but off we tramped. We had wellies, rain coat, 'sou'wester' (like John West on the salmon tins) and our bags on our backs. We always attempted to climb up the usual route in mud and water. If we didn't manage we went a little to the left and clinging to sods of grass we tried to climb up. If we had to give up we went up the Knock towards the present Kennedy Park and approached school via the front of St Aidan's Crescent.

In the CBS we had second class to sixth class. I think Brother Kelleher and later Brother Gleason was the principal in my day. It was in the CBS that new friendships were forged. We now met up with lads who had been to the Mercy and The Faythe schools. We also encountered male teachers for the first time. In fact there were no female teachers in the CBS. There we also met teachers who had come to Wexford from all corners of the country. There seemed to be an uneven amount from Kerry.

I cannot recall who taught me during those days in the CBS primary. I recall Paddy Ryan was there but I was never in his class. There was Brother English who was mad about GAA – not the only one. I remember him because I got an old English sixpence for scoring a goal in an inter-class football match in the field behind the school. Mind you it's the only game I ever remember playing in. I think there was also a Mr. Stack from Kerry.

Outside the academic, there were the games of course. 'Tig Den' was very popular as was the game of 'jack stones'. We hear a lot these days about the walloping people got in school. To be honest I cannot recall excesses. Oh there were the 'leathers' alright and we all got our share – fair or otherwise – of leathering. Mind you I think they used the psychology of having you line up to await punishment to great effect. For some weird reason we went to Green Street for second and third classes, then for

Above left:

The Seal of the Bridge Commissioners.

Above right:

This picture taken in The Faythe a century ago may depict a normal delivery from a shop but the baskets remind us of those used by lightship men for provisions. (Lawrence Collection)

Right: This is the first page of a reproduction of the act to improve the quays.

Anno Regni tricesimo quarto

Georgii III. Regis.

C H A P. XXVI.

An Act for the Improvement of the Town and Harbour of *Wexford*, and for building a Bridge or Bridges over the River *Slaney*, at or near said Town.

WHEREAS the Bar or Entrance into the Harbour of Wexford, is exceedingly dangerous and unsafe, by Reason of the Shallowness of the Water thereon, whereby many Vessels have been lost or otherwise much damaged, which might be remedied by confining the Water, and deepening one or more Channel or Channels, and the Trade of said Town would be much benefited by the making, erecting, and extending One or more Quay or Quays along the said Town, from Saint Paul's Quay, to the Ferry Boat Quay, or to where a Bridge shall
8 L   be

fourth we had to trek to George's Street. I cannot recall the genius behind this idea. It was like going back in time to the old two-room schoolhouse of the country and the past. Funnily enough it is the year I remember best. The teacher I didn't have was Mr. O'Gara and anyone who didn't have him felt left out because he told stories on Fridays. I cannot recall our teacher's name. He was a brother and was stone mad on singing Marnalaigh *Sinn a Chairde* still haunts me. In George's Street we had semi-central heating – pot bellied stoves that provided more smoke than heat at times were situated in each class. The toilet blocks were outside and either side of the front yard was below the level of the concrete, giving us twin lakes in wet weather.

Just as we had Holy Communion towards the end of convent school, Confirmation came as we were in sixth class in the CBS. There was great consternation learning the catechism. It had questions graded as blue, red and black in order of difficulty. We were driven mad as we waited for the bishop to come and test us on our religious knowledge. There were tales of being barred from Confirmation if you gave a wrong answer. We had been primed for this in a way each year during the primary schooling when Father Anglim arrived to question us on the catechism. Weeks were spent ignoring reading, writing and sums, as his visit grew nearer. Another visit that saw manic preparation was that of the 'inspector'. We always trembled about this coming – little did we realise that it wasn't the pupil being inspected but the teacher.

Primary schooling ended in July after we sat our first exam – The Primary Cert. It is hard to believe that this was such an important exam of English, Irish and Arithmetic (we still had not discovered maths). Many lads left school at that point so that was their only certificate.

Here we have a group photograph after a concert by six and seven year olds at the Presentation School in about 1958. (Rossiter Collection)

This picture of boats drawn up on the sand at the Cott Safe off Batt Street reminds us of the seafaring traditions of Wexford. Even into the present day many residents of that area retain their boats. (Rossiter Collection)

SECONDARY SCHOOL

The secondary education saw a few alternatives. You might continue with the brothers. Some headed for St Peter's College and a few – a very few - headed off to boarding school. In those days there was no free secondary education and we had sat 'scholarship examinations' to get some financial help from the County Council with the fees. I have a slight recollection of the fees being 12/6 per term but I cannot swear to it. That was quite an amount out a Pierce's pay packet back then. I entered an ESB scholarship contest and wrote a composition (now called essays) about the hydroelectric scheme at Ardnacrusha. I think I won something for that. I think it was in that first year in secondary that I met John Beakey whose father owned the pub now known as The Pike. I also met Declan Sinnott, John Morgan and Dick Doyle in those years along with Ray Murphy and most of the other names I still recall from school.

The teachers were again a mixture of brothers, established local teachers and new teachers fresh from college. There was a Mr. Murphy, I think, from Kerry again who fell into the latter category. I recall one of my school pals actually confronting him at one stage over some dispute in class. I remember his name but I won't divulge it.

In secondary school we started exotic new subjects. Latin was one of these. I only appreciate this subject long after the struggles of reading Virgil and the Punic Wars. One of the teachers of that language was referred to as 'Mensa' because that Latin word for table was one of the first we learned. Another was called Jinx but I haven't a clue as to why. He also ran the school shop. No we didn't have a 'tuck shop' like those in the English comics. This shop only sold our schoolbooks and copies. Who remembers that bloody big Irish grammar book with the covers like vinyl?

Mr. Martin Murphy taught us bookkeeping and business studies (I still know what FOC means) he was a brother of Canon Murphy I think and was always chatty with lads from Glynn, Joe Cullen was given the task of explaining science. Mr. Sweetman taught us geography and was a great man to digress and make the whole lesson more interesting. The Bear taught another subject but I cannot recall which, I do remember that he grew grapes in the greenhouse of the Monastery. 'Hoss' taught English. The one comment I recall from this man had nothing to do with Shakespeare but was the phrase used as a pupil with bad posture passed the window – "here's me head, me arse is following". See how good an education is?

The brother who taught us history was probably my least favourite. I cannot recall his name but he was a very sarcastic man and it is ironic that although he turned me against 'the hundred years war', I now love social history.

A TOUR

Walks into Our Past

To understand and appreciate Wexford, one should take time to stroll around, look and absorb its story. Where to start is always a problem, followed by how long do you want to walk. To facilitate the latter we will divide the walk into sections that need not tax either the stamina or the mind in taking in too much information. We will have a tour of the quays and of the commercial heart of Wexford, past and present and also a stroll in the suburbs or side streets.

The Quays

Let us start in an unusual place. We walk halfway on to the bridge over the Slaney from Ferrybank. From here we see that the town is built on a series of shelves – Quay, Main Street, High Street etc. Wexford author and playwright Billy Roche described Wexford as 'tumbling down' to the waterfront and used the phrase as the title of his novel about the town and its characters.

Take a minute to look to the left of our new skyscraper hotel and admire the steeples of the twin churches built in the decade after The Famine or St Peter's College on a height above the town. St Peters is the large building in the background. Just to the left is a cluster of religion. The high spire is Rowe Street or the Church of the Immaculate Conception. To the left of that is the square tower of the Franciscan Friary and almost hidden in the foreground between them is the steeple of St Iberius Church. The other 'twin' is further off to the left.

To the right of the bridge at low tide you may see the ribs of an old boat. This was the Maria Reid a sailing ship, a relic of a maritime past now rotting in an estuary that silted up the harbour and extinguished a seafaring tradition. The rocks to be seen there may be remnants of 'Selskar' or 'seal rock' to which a causeway is said to have connected the site of Selskar Abbey. The site of the proposed inshore rescue station is between the bridge and the railway goods yard. This is an ironic site because it

At low tide the remains of the Maria Reid are in the foreground in this view from the bridge. In the middle distance is Selskar Rock. (Rossiter Collection)

This scene is just to the right of the bridge entering town. It has since been filled in where the boats lie. The building is part of the railway goods yard. The concrete area beside its wall is the site of a shed where bodies recovered from the harbour were kept in a building to await inquest. (Rossiter Collection)

was in the 'Deddery' here that bodies recovered from the harbour were held awaiting identification or inquest. This townscape is changing rapidly and utterly with new developments. Wexford has seldom stood still.

Stepping left onto the wide majestic quayfront you are walking where only ten years ago was water. The modern quay front is hundreds of metres from the original shoreline. At this point the shore was back up as far as the top of Charlotte Street that is opposite you.

Before we proceed south along the quay look seaward. Out there in the distance are Ardcavan and the reclaimed South Sloblands, sweeping around to the point of The Raven. In earlier times the harbour was dotted with islands and shallows and mudflats.

The approach to the bridge at Ferrybank reveals the remnant of the old oak bridge abutment. The name Ferrybank refers to the site of a ferry prior to the building of the Oak Bridge in 1794. The present bridge opened in 1959 but was closed and completely resurfaced – down to the support piers – in 1997.

The fields at Ferrybank were known as The Dairy Fields and were a popular courting location into the middle of the twentieth century before they were turned into a caravan park and a small arbouretum of trees planted annually by the celebrities performing the official opening of the Wexford Festival Opera. In the near foreground is the mooring place for mussel boats that was established when the quay was being widened and stretching southward is the breakwater culminating in the 'Black Man'. The Breakwater was constructed on the instructions of the Harbour Commissioners in the middle of the nineteenth century to protect the inner harbour. The Black Man is a navigation aid as well as the terminal for the Breakwater.

Let us turn inland and stroll the quay. This side of the road is probably the best vantage point to appreciate the buildings on the quay. Walking the quay until the late

The bridge was stripped down to the piers a few years ago. (Rossiter Collection)

The Woodenworks under construction. (Lawrence Collection)

twentieth century gave you a wonderful sight as you could have motor traffic on the road, a train proceeding along the tracks and a boat cruising the water. All would have been within ten metres of each other as you walked the Woodenworks or Pilewharf. That Woodenworks was a unique waterfront walk along planks six or eight inches thick with the harbour waters lapping ten feet below. The edifice was constructed in the late 1800s but not to carry the railway through the town to Rosslare Harbour as is commonly believed. The main railway was always on the solid quay front. The Woodenworks was built to allow wagons to be shunted close to the hundreds of boats unloading here to take the cargoes of coal, timber and a myriad of other goods. It is important to note that where we now walk was not generally open to the public a century ago. It was a working port with all the restrictions, dangers and policing required for what was in essence a factory or industrial site.

It should be borne in mind that a linear quayfront dates only from around the early 1800s in Wexford. Prior to that quays or wharves were at right angles to the waterfront and were usually private edifices allowing merchants to land good at the rear of their premises. The quay here is called Commercial Quay, which indicates its primary purpose in the past. We shall encounter a number of such names as we proceed along the waterfront as the purpose and usage changed.

In 1798, executions were carried out on the oaken bridge built near the current bridge four years previously. Both sides engaged in the bloodbath, with bodies being flung into the river and heads mounted on spikes. Directly opposite the end of the bridge stood the courthouse. It was built in 1805 replacing one at the Bullring. It was destroyed by three explosions and a fire at 2.00 am on 18 June 1921, during the War of Independence. A portion of the building at the rear was left intact and was later used as a Scout Hall for the Second Wexford CBSI. This group vacated the hall for

These two machines were part of an array of such items that spanned the working quayside of Wexford into the 1990s. (Rossiter Collection)

modernised premises at Clifford Street in 1962. It was proposed to build a dance hall on the courthouse site in 1961, but the plan was abandoned. A Service Station later occupied the site and during its construction, some of the piles used for supporting the courthouse were unearthed. They are stated to have been in excellent condition over a century and a half later. This area is now a carpark. In keeping with the port, this area of Commercial Quay once housed Kinsellas Coalyard.

On the corner of Charlotte Street there is an auctioneers office. An interesting point to note is the recessed or 'cut off' lower corner of the building. This was common in the days of coach travel when control of the horses was not always possible and the wheels often clipped buildings. The interestingly named Entiknapp's sold sweets, ices and tobacco in this shop in the early 1900s. The shop to its right was a chip shop run by Turner's in the late 1900s. Pierce Turner the singer/songwriter is of that family.

Across Charlotte Street is a wonderful little building, now surrounded by The Centenary Stores. It was possibly a post office in the 1800s and was the premises of Doyle's Plumbers in the 1900s.

The new façade of The Centenary Stores facing the quay replaces a wonderful old building where Kevin Morris, many times mayor of Wexford, had his auctioneering business. Prior to that it was the first premises of McCormack Brothers, hardware and earlier still it was Breen's Ironmongers.

Mooney's premises were previously Kinsellas – the same family as the Coalyard.

The tall building next door was the original Provincial Bank before it moved in 1880 to Anne Street corner. Hugh McGuire then acquired it as ships chandlers.

A detail from a Lawrence Collection photograph shows not only a beautiful sailing ship, once so common in the harbour, but also the courthouse when it stood opposite the present bridge.

At the bottom of Charlotte Street we find the corner recessed to avoid contact with coach wheels at a time when this was part of the mail coach route. (Rossiter Collection)

The low building to the right of the boat is still used into the 21ˢᵗ century. It may once have been a post office but when this picture was taken it was a plumbing business of Mr. Doyle. (Lawrence Collection)

The narrow lane behind the iron gate is one of our oldest and most mysterious. It is known as Roman Lane although we never had any record of a Roman settlement. In some English towns Roman Lane denoted a lane or street where Roman Catholics had places of worship during the early centuries of the Reformation. The lane was only three feet wide and extended to the Main Street but the top end was incorporated into buildings.

Shaw's now backs onto the quays and replaces a few smaller buildings that stood there into the late 1900s. In the 1930s one was Rogers shop selling bicycles and wirelesses and another was a furniture store run by Billy Rackard one of the three legendary Rackard brothers of the mid-twentieth century Wexford hurling team. Look at that archway and the legend for O'Connor's Steam Bakery. It tells its own story.

To the south is lovely old small pub. Many of these dotted the quays in the past. They were probably the first and last port of call for thirsty seamen. This one was once called The Keyhole Bar indicating the small size.

The present ESB yard was the hub of a major shipping business. Here Harry Wilson operated his shipping and coal importing business. He was also a Lloyd's agent. The shipping connection of the site went back to Gaffney's who earlier had a coal and iron yard there.

The two premises leading to the corner have a wonderful facade recalling that these were originally one building and part of the St Iberius Club that ran up most of Common Quay Street.

We are now on Common Quay. This was thought to recall something similar to common land but from recent research it may just be the quay adjacent to the old Common Plain or Bullring. In times past all quays were privately owned and operated. The Common Quay may have been an access point for the ordinary sailor or small boat to dock and load or unload. The 1970s architecture of the Bank of Ireland stands on the former coal and wool yard of Ffrenche's and an old malt store. Keane's Auctioneers is

Today Roman Lane is behind a timber door that stops us appreciating this old narrow thoroughfare. (Rossiter Collection)

The old rear entrance to Fran O'Connor's Steam Bakery. (Rossiter Collection)

The sign just to the left of the sail identifies Cecelia Gaffney's yard. (Lawrence Collection)

housed in a beautifully kept old building. It was built as The Union Club around 1830 and later became The Commercial Club.

Another quaint pub The Wrens Nest is located next door. It was once smaller but it took in the veterinary stables of Staples.

Now we come to one of our many Wexford anomalies. The development here is called Key West — yes it is spelt Key and has no Wexford connection. The primary feature here used to be the narrow exit of Church Lane running directly from the Main Street to the quays. Before the new development that lane opened out on to a large car park. Prior to that use the quay end had housed the stores section of Wexford Corporation.

Cooper's Solicitors also had offices in the area. Boggan's Garage fronted the quay here and the workshop stretched up parallel to Church Lane. We are now on Custom House Quay. The lovely building occupied by Southeast Radio was formerly the National Bank. The carved head over the door reminds us of the artistic architecture of such buildings in the past. To the right of the door was the entrance to a garden at the rear of the bank. It was built over in the 1900s.

To the south of the bank were Thompson's sawmills and hardware shops. These later became McCormack & Hegarty's and then McCormack's housing the same type of business. Joyce's store on the quay was the original home of Hardob's Textile Factory when it set up in Wexford in the 1960s before moving to the Industrial Estate at Whitemill.

At the corner of Anne Street was English's Printing Works. This was one of a number of printers in Wexford in the twentieth century. It produced mainly jobbing printing but also excelled at book production and was the printer of the Capuchin Annual among others for many years. The red brick building on the opposite side was the Provincial Bank from around 1880. It is now part of Wexford Credit Union.

This view shows the end of
Common Quay Street, the St.
Iberius Club and Harry Wilson's
yard. Note the fantastic tower on
the Friary in the left background.
(Lawrence Collection)

Observe the rounded roof on the adjoining building. Walsh and Corish of Taghmon moved here in 1918 with an auctioneering business and the trade continues to this day.

Next door was George Murphy's Garage with petrol pumps at the kerb and an enamel plate with a map of Ireland attached to the wall. To the rear was Allen's timber yard in the 1800s. It is now offices for Wexford County Council. The lane here is Cullimore's Lane and probably takes its name from the original owner. The old Bank of Ireland building dating from 1835 leads us round on to Crescent Quay. This quay referred to in a document of the early 1800s as 'Elliptical Quay' is situated on the old Deep Pool of Wexford. We will leave the quayfront and walk the waterside crescent.

The next building along is Asple's Public House. It may have been one of the hundreds of malt stores that dotted Wexford in the 18th and 19th centuries. Sleggs lane opens off the car park to the rear – we will look at this from the Main Street.

Donovan's Wharf is the name given to the regenerated buildings from the car park entrance.

These replace some old premises that survived into the late 1900s. First was Underwood's who appear to have been very varied in their trade offering everything from tinsmith through bicycles to undertaking. Beside this was a timber yard that was owned by Staffords and earlier by Ennis. One of my favourite building here was formerly Browne's Forge. It was an establishment for shoeing horses and ponies. It later housed Bookends, one of our first second-hand bookshops and was run by Jimmy Lacey.

The magnificent archway beside Donovan's Wharf is just that, an archway. It leads to the goods entrance for Penney's stores on South Main Street. The building

This was the Union Club. (Rossiter Collection)

This head recalls when the building was
The National Bank. (Rossiter Collection)

Into the 1950s timber could be imported directly to the quayside. Here we see a consignment being unloaded for McCormack & Hegarty whose retail premises are just across the road from the boat. A handcart is sufficient for transport. Behind the man in the brown shop coat ticking off the load we can see a railway wagon. These wagons were shunted on to the Woodenworks and took loads from the boats for longer transhipment. (Rossiter Collection)

The old Provincial Bank in Anne Street. (Rossiter Collection)

on the corner of Henrietta Street is The Ballast Office. It was built as headquarters of the Harbour Commissioners in the 1800s. They still use the premises but it also houses a number of other businesses. An interesting feature is the apparent carvings of the window ledges. It is said that the shapes were made by sailors using the sills to sharpen their knives.

Crescent Mall is the row of shops dividing Henrietta Street from Harpur's Lane. They are built on the old Stafford's Sawmill and timber yard. The rear of Tesco is built on the old Talbot Garage. The entry to the carpark here once was a lane leading to Wickham's Brewery on South Main Street. Take some time to admire two lovely old houses, still residences, from an old Wexford. The slate fronts protect against rain.

On the corner here is one of the many customhouses that operated in Wexford as the port thrived. It once hade a 'belvedere' or small glass area in the roof where the officers could observe ships using the port.

As we step back on to the quayfront let us look back towards the statute of John Barry on the Crescent. The statue was unveiled in September 1956 by President, Sean T. O'Kelly, having been transported via Rosslare Harbour on board the US destroyer *Charles S. Perry*. In June of each year the United States government and local and national bodies honour this founder of the American Navy, born at Ballysampson about 10 miles south of Wexford. The ceremony also commemorates the Wexford sailors lost during conflicts. (See also The Miscellany section).

We are now on Paul Quay. This title is variously attributed to Paul Turner a landowner in earlier times. An alternative is that the original title was 'The Quay of the Pale' or Pale Quay. This latter name is shown in a document dated 1610. Pale is another name for a fort or fortress and seems fitting when one considers the proximity of both Wexford Castle and Stafford's Castle.

Another grain store dating from around 1900 called Old Mill House stood beside the customhouse. It was demolished overnight in the late 1900s. The lane here is Oyster Lane. It was a lane with a number of hotels and inns back in the 1800s. Carr's was the more prominent offering oysters, brown bread and porter as a specialty. Oysters were a common commodity in those times and were regular fare for the common people.

Along Paul Quay, now undergoing development stood the offices of Stafford's. They were ship owners, importers, exporters and much else besides. The buildings along here dating from 1936 housed the coal import and sales section in the 1900s. It was here that we went to order coal for household delivery. The yards were huge and they had their own weighbridge. It was in this vicinity that the company's ships had their cargoes of coal, timber and goods of all description unloaded for it's many enterprises. Stafford's were the last major sailing ship owners in Wexford and had sail-making lofts on this quay. The Stafford family bought their first steamships in 1919, named Elsie Annie after a daughter, and the 'J.F.V.' (James, Francis, Victor) after their sons. By the outbreak of war in 1939, they operated the most modern fleet in Ireland under the title of the Wexford Steamship Co.

The stone built wall beside the railway tracks here represents the original outfall of the Bishopswater River into the harbour. Pierce Court is a new development. Once again it is on the site of some interesting old buildings. Pierces Foundry had a social club for its employees in this area. It was on these premises that the tontine society was introduced to Wexford from France where the company had offices. The system entailed members paying a fixed sum each week and withdrawing the savings at times

Coffins. Coffins. Coffins.

THOMAS UNDERWOOD

Begs to announce that he has started full Undertaking business, and will supply the very best Oak, Pitch Pine and Deal Coffins on shortest notice and at lowest possible prices. Everything will be executed in the most up-to-date style Superior quality. Best workmanship All orders receive personal attention.

THOMAS UNDERWOOD, PLUMBER, TIN AND COPPER SMITH, CYCLE AGENT, ETC.,

CRESCENT QUAY AND FAYTHE, WEXFORD.

Underwood's advertisement in 1917.

such as Christmas. In addition, when a member died, each subscriber gave a small sum called a 'death' and the money collected was put towards the burial costs. It sounds like a very simple matter today but at a time before credit cards, credit unions and easy loans when fear of a pauper's grave haunted many, it was a great and very popular idea.

An adjoining building was used to store finished implements from the foundry awaiting shipment and also the coke and pig iron imported for the industry. Howard Rowe had a flourmill here too and at one time the Sisters of Mercy provided 'penny dinners' to the poor of the town from a premises on Paul Quay.

There were a number of pubs here in the not too distant past including The Harbour Bar. A hostel for staff of The Talbot Hotel was also located here. The pub on the corner continues a tradition of pubs on the site. If we continue along the waterfront through the car park we come to the site where the old steam packet passenger ship left on its regular sailings. Looking seaward again and slightly to the north we see a rather curious man-made island in the harbour opposite Paul Quay. This is The Ballast Bank. It was erected in 1831 to provide a place loading an unloading the ballast essential to stabilize ships sailing without cargo. Prior to that the ballast was stored on ballast wharfs on the quay.

The window ledge of the Ballast Office. (Rossiter Collection)

These lovely old houses with slate fronts are still occupied and face on The Crescent.
(Rossiter Collection)

117

Above: The Woodenworks as they looked up to the 1990s at The Crescent.

Below: This is The Talbot Hotel circa the 1930s.

THE MAIN STREET

We retrace our steps to that pub on the corner and head away from the sea and up King Street. The Corporation tried to call it Partridge street in 1920 but apart from the name plaque it never caught on. The street has been redeveloped in recent times replacing the many malt stores that would have lined it. At the top we turn right on to the Main Street but what we are entering is called Stonebridge. The actual bridge is about 100 metres from the corner and was until recently delineated by a tarmacadam strip. In the

118

It is surprising how few Wexford people have seen the town from the sea. This picture from the early 1970s shows Trinity Street. The old South Station stood in the foreground. Only the signal box remained at the time. On the extreme right is one of the old gas tanks of Wexford Gas Consumers Ltd. (Rossiter Collection)

past it has been called Wexford Bridge and in 1764 it was known as Jew's Bridge. The bridge was built over the Bishopswater River and may have marked the northern gate of the earliest Norse or V king settlement.

The first recorded story of murder or manslaughter in Wexford Town happened at Stonebridge. At about mid-afternoon on 25 February 1560, a quarrel took place between Thomas Walsh, a shoemaker, and Geoffrey Brian, a mariner. The insults led to blows being exchanged and finally Brian stabbed Walsh below the heart. Walsh died from the wounds received.

On our left entering this street is a new development on the site of the old Capitol Cinema. Staffords Furniture Store stood here at the beginning of the twentieth century. The Capitol Cinema opened on Sunday 15 February 1931, with a film called *The Big Trail* The adjoining premises once popularly known as Joe Dillon's were a venue for popular entertainment including bingo sessions. The Capitol was the second purpose built cinema to open in the town but was also used as a concert venue. Among those who appeared at the Capitol, were Jack Doyle and Movita (she later married Marlon Brando) in January 1944, and in 1945 the Wexford Theatre Players with *Variety Spotlight* starring Martin Crosby and Cecil Sheridan. The cinema queues often stretched around the corner into King Street, and were kept in order by the cries of 'Two Deep Now — Two Deep' coming from a cinema attendant. A notable character of the time was Tommy Swift, he was a man of low stature, who sold newspapers from a little pram-cum-handcart to people who queued at the Capitol Cinema. The Capitol closed in the early 1990s.

Opposite the Capitol is O'Toole's. It is now an antique shop but in the mid to late 1900s it was a very popular gathering place for young people. There they sat for hours over 'bottles of minerals', ice cream sundaes or cups of coffee. The front of the shop was an Aladdin's Cave of exotic tobacco products, Swiss army knives and toys. The Capitol Bar, now a Chinese restaurant, was a popular venue for a pint before of after a visit to the cinema.

Turning right at Stonebridge we find Larkin's Lane, also known as Sinnott's Place. In the early 1900s the right hand side of this lane accommodated Stafford's offices, and provision cellars. On the other side there was a forge. The Larkin name derived

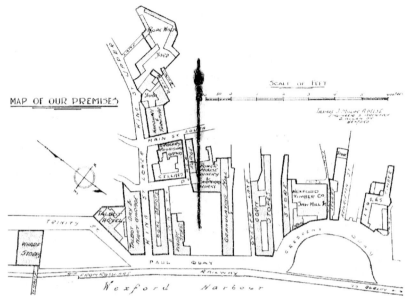

MAP OF OUR PREMISES

This sketch map gives us an idea of the extensive holdings of Staffords, particularly around South Main Street. The ship wharf and store is on the left. Their hardware and furniture store faces a provisions store with cellars across the main street. There is a forge, powerhouse and carpentry works in Sinnotts Lane.

Looking above the shop fronts is always a rewarding experience in an old town. These beautiful decorations are above Hera at Oyster Lane. (Rossiter Collection)

120

This is a fantastic view of Coffey's Hill from the 1950s. Note the Temperance Hotel and the sign for Mrs Dempsey's Tea Rooms. The child in the foreground is being wheeled up the hill in a tansad – at least that's what we called them. The boot sign outside Coffeys is a throwback to the old days of illiteracy when signs told the story of the goods on offer.

from an extensive bakery, which came later. The bakery is long gone and the premises became home to Wexford's Theatre Workshop in the 1980s. Windmill Therapeutic now occupy the site. A generator was housed in the lane, which provided electrical power for Stafford's Enterprises between 1921 and 1928. It was Wexford's first major electrical plant.

To the left at Stonebridge is Stonebridge Lane. It was called 'The Hole of The Wreck' in the past. In 1800s there were 27 houses listed there. James Prendergast who also lived in the lane owned the majority. Moving north along South Main Street we pass shops on the right built on the site of Staffords Castle. This Castle was owned by Stafford, the man who by tradition betrayed Wexford to Cromwell. It became a gaol in 1665 and was used to house prisoners during the 1798 rebellion. In 1812 a new gaol was built at Spawell Road and the castle became a Lunatic Asylum and House of Industry. As such it housed the aged and infirm and also vagrants and prostitutes. Inmates of the House of Industry were often employed in cleaning the streets. The castle was eventually demolished in 1866 to provide land for development. Where Bride Street joins Main Street on our left was known as Coffin Corner in 1812.

This may stem from a time when military personnel from Wexford Castle were buried in St Mary's graveyard and passed along this way. From the building of the twin churches until excess traffic caused rerouting it would have earned the name again as funerals from Bride Street Church usually went this way on to Main Street and the

121

quays. An older red brick house on this corner was home to one of the many tontine societies in the town in the 1900s. During excavation for the building now standing to the north of this junction, evidence of our Viking past was uncovered. Similar remnants were found at Oyster Lane almost opposite. The Xtravision shop opposite Bride Street is on the site of Murphy's Clay Pipe Factory. I also recall Barry's fish shop on the site.

At the top of Oyster Lane was Malone's fish shop where a cat was often to be seen sunning itself in the window. On the opposite corner of Oyster Lane the Pettit supermarket empire started in about 1947. The original house was the birthplace of Father James Roche, driving force in the construction of Wexford's twin churches.

Where the modern toilet is there was once the old style, manned public convenience on the corner of Mann's Lane.

The Dun Mhuire entertainment complex opened in 1960 in premises with a varied history. The Devereux family owned it over a hundred years ago. It was the residence of the clergy of the church of the Assumption until 1889. Later it became a barracks for the Royal Irish Constabulary, and with Irish Independence it housed the Civic Guards who later moved to Roche's Road. The local branch of the Legion of Mary started here in 1934 and acquired the building in 1938. The Legion operated a Catholic Girls Club there.

Opposite Dun Mhuire is a hairdresser. It was here that Jem Roche a favourite for the title of World Heavyweight Boxing Champion in 1908 operated a public house. The advertising motto was 'Only Champion Drinks Served'. The 147 Club was a pub called the Long Room and is situated on the site of the old Wickham's Brewery. Lowney's Mall offers an array of shops on what some readers will recall as one long shop called The Universal Stores. There John and Peggy Lowney helped many of our parents and grandparents to fit out that new corporation house – there were not too many mortgages then. It was opened on the site of a bakery owned by one-time Mayor of Wexford, Mr. Howard Rowe.

The shops on the side opposite are those of Colman Doyle who started with a small hardware shop beside Heffernan's in the late 1900s. It is fascinating to recall Colman starting out with his little hardware shop where once stood Stephen Doyle's and earlier Sinnotts Bacon Shop. His by-word was 'If we haven't got it, we will get it for you.' Heffernan's pub is on the site of Hay's Castle. Walter Hay was recorded as living in Wexford in 1641. The street next to it is Peter Street, known locally as Gibson's Lane. The name came from William Gibson who had the malt store at the corner. It is one of the named streets as Gibson's Lane in 1764.

Directly opposite Peter Street is what the locals call Cinema Lane. The lane has officially been named Moran's Lane, Harpur's Lane and Hay's Lane. The more commonly used name comes from the Palace Cinema that was opened in the lane on 7 December 1914. The first concert performance was in aid of Belgian refugees of the Great War. The Hay's Lane name is from Hay's Castle which stood on the corner of Gibson's Street where Heffernan's Pub is now located. It has the name Moran's Lane in a map of around 1812. The cinema was opened in a former bonded warehouse where The Receiver of Wrecks stored goods salvaged from shipwrecks before they were auctioned. The title of Harpur's Lane comes from Francis Harpur, businessman, ship owner and Lloyd's agent who lived here in 1827. He was also a town councilor and three times mayor of Wexford. In 1853 Francis Harpur had a ship store here. In our youth, Cinema Lane was the focal point of our Saturday and Sunday afternoon

This is the last remnant of a house of dreams that was the Cinema Palace. The Roche Decorators of the sign is also a part of history.
(Rossiter Collection)

with mind trips to New York, the Wild West and Africa, courtesy of Mrs. Latimer and the staff of The Palace. If we were old enough or lucky enough to get to the weeknight pictures the next treat as chips at Kevin Roche's on South Main Street with enamel plates and the long narrow poster telling us what to expect next week at the pictures – never the cinema. I suppose today, if the Palace had survived, we could prolong the American fantasy with burgers and more in Uncle Sams. Peter Murphy's shop was on this site and Nick Murphy's pub next door was where the thirsty printers of The Free Press needed a well-earned drink after producing your weekly newspaper?

The slight incline here on South Main Street is known as Coffey's Hill and actually gives the title to a piece of popular music played by St Patrick's Fife and Drum Band which was founded in Wexford in 1893. The shop in question, Coffeys, stood where Heaton's now trade. It was a family store that traded for over a century on this site selling clothes, footwear and nursery products in the latter years. The premises were the Hat and Cap Warehouse in 1877. Coffey's also owned the pawnshop managed by and colloquially referred to as Davy Tobin's in Abbey Street into the 1960s.

Opposite Coffeys was The Temperance Hotel. These were common throughout the British Isles in the late 1800s and early 1900s. Miss Maggie Dempsey operated a wonderful second-hand book and comic store in this area in the mid 1900s. It was there that many people made the acquaintance of Dan Dare, Flash Gordon, Batman and Superman among others. With emigration came a few benefits. Aunts and uncles in Britain and the U.S.A. often included these comics in the parcels home. The comics then began a circular journey through the hands and minds of countless Wexford children thanks to Maggie's emporium.

The street leading to the quay here is Henrietta Street. This is a street of wh ch little remains from twenty years ago, much less its industries of two hundred years past, including the coach factory. A little further along on the left Allen Street branches

JOHN SINNOTT & SONS,

MANUFACTURING IRONMONGERS,

Cabinet Makers, Undertakers, and Upholsterers,

BELL HANGERS, SMITHS, AND GENERAL PLUMBERS,
IMPLEMENT AGENTS AND SEED MERCHANTS.

All kinds of Hydraulic Engines, Baths, Lavatories, W.C.'s, Kitchen Ranges, &c., erected.
Bar, Rod and Sheet Iron; Steel, Copper and Zinc; Galvanised Roofing, Chains and Nails, Ropes and Cords, Paints, Oils and Colours, &c., &c.
A large and well-assorted Stock of Furniture, Carpets and Hearth Rugs; Toilet, Pier, and Chimney Glasses, Lamps, Cutlery, Sheffield and Electro-plated Ware, Linoleum and Oilcloths, &c., &c.

ESTIMATES ON APPLICATION.   ORDERS PROMPTLY ATTENDED TO.

29 SOUTH MAIN STREET, *Wexford.* 21st April 1913

Above: This is letterhead from the business of John Sinnott in 1913.

Left: Here is another Wexford building that eschewed the typical square front. Paddy Lyons sold shoes and is reputed to have been the first shop in town to have plastic carrier bags with the shop name printed. (Rossiter Collection)

This is Anne Street in the 1970s. On the right is the County Hotel and further down on the same side is the old government building, since completely rebuilt.
(Rossiter Collection)

Looking towards the Bullring from Fettitt's Lane. (Lawrence Collection)

125

west from Main Street. It is named after the Rev. Joseph Allen. It was known as Broad Street in 1649 and was paved first in 1793. In 1824 Corbett and Rochford's Ladies Boarding School was located in this street. John Hickey was master of a post office in Allen Street in 1824. In *Pigot's Directory* of that year it is noted that mail from Dublin arrived at 10.15 am and was dispatched at 3.30 pm and letters were to be posted by 3 o'clock. Mail from Broadway (South of the town) arrived every Sunday, Wednesday and Friday at 10am.

At the corner of Allen Street was Nolan's sweet shop and cafe, which was a popular meeting place for the youth of the town over the years. Here they listened to the latest hit records played on the jukebox. On the right corner was The Wexford Brass and Iron Foundry. An old lane called Kenny's was incorporated into Hore's Stores beside Penney's. It exited in the lower section of Henrietta Street. At number thirty-one South Main Street now part of Hore's drapery business, Edward Walsh established *The People Newspaper* in 1853. It incorporated the *Wexford Guardian* of the previous year. *The People* went from strength to strength and is still published in Wexford albeit at another location. Hores was famous in the mid 1900s for its rhyming advertisements in the local newspapers.

Penney's department store is on the site of Kenny's Hall where Oliver Cromwell is said to have stayed for a short time in October 1649 after the fall of Wexford. The current store replaced Woolworth's in the 1980s. Kenny's Hall is believed to have been a castellated mansion, perhaps of medieval origin. During the Confederate War David Sinnott, the Military Governor of Wexford, lived there. The name Kenny's Hall dates from the 1700s when the Kenny family lived there. An alderman of the town Mr. Sinnott took a lease on the building in the 1840s and operated a very successful hardware, undertaking and cabinet making business on the premises.

In 1870 Richard Devereux purchased the head rent on the building and bequeathed it to the Society of the St Vincent De Paul. The hardware business continued under Frank Gaul until just before the arrival of Woolworth's when major renovation and re-modeling was carried out.

Barkers Shop incorporates two interesting old Wexford shops. One was the giftware store that gives its name, Barkers. As well as giftware you could book sea passages there in the early 1900s, the shop was established in 1843 as Marine Stores again reminding us of our maritime past. The other shop was Paddy Lyons shoe shop. This is reputed to be the first Wexford shop giving plastic bags with the shop name printed on it.

Fitzgerald's store was the hardware, seed and ammunition shop of S& R Pierce until the 1980s. This was a huge old style hardware shop full of nooks and crannies, big counters and brushes and shovels hung outside throughout the day.

Sleggs Lane on the seaward side is one of my favourite lanes in Wexford or anywhere else. It is entered via a low arch opposite Fitzgerald's shop. One then descends a short flight of steps under the shops to emerge into a car park. In earlier timers one would continue down the narrow thoroughfare to the Deep Pool or Crescent Quay. In October 1866 this lane was one three mentioned as being in a filthy state and a danger to public health with cholera in the town. This lane still gives a real feel of old Wexford.

Keysar's Lane, beside Fitzgerald's is one of our oldest lanes and it is often confused with Slegg's Lane. Keysar's Lane joins South Main Street to High Street. It was called Keizar's in Griffith's Chronicles in 1764. Tradition tells the lovely story that the name

This is Whelan's pub on North Main Street in the 1940s. You can see the name Foresters Hall above the Corish Memorial Hall – Richard Corish was still alive at this time.

This was one of the major drapery shops on North Main Street into the late 1900s. (Rossiter Collection)

Looking from The Bullring towards the north. (Lawrence Collection)

derives from 'kiss arse lane' because the steepness caused people to fall on their rears or be in a position to kiss the posterior of those in front when climbing the lane. Today, we have a car park where many houses once stood in this lane. In 1853 there were 25 premises recorded here, primarily houses with yards. Among the inhabitants were Ba Swift and Nicholas Murphy, a baker's oven keeper. Just along this so-called 'golden mile' of retail Wexford there were some fabulous shops in the past.

Charlie Pierce's shop is on the site of one of our first chippers where the appropriately named Mr. Fisher sold fish and chips and ice cream. We also had the L&N here. That was the London & Newcastle Tea Company reminding us of our colonial past.

Doyle's Butchers replaces Matty Furlongs where Wexfordians including the fledgling St Bridget's Fife & Drum Band bought musical instruments, sheet music and wallpaper among other items into the mid 1900s. We had Allie Whites where we were treated if we behaved well, to an ice cream sundae. I also remember lovely spearmint bars without a makers name but they had a sort of cobweb design on the wrapper.

Healy and Collins Department Store where RTV now does business were renowned among the youngsters at least for the innovative cash system. Little boxes flew back and forth on wires throughout the shop. Cash was put into the container and whizzed off to the office where a receipt and change were inserted and returned to the counter and

Here we have another piece of old Wexford that disappeared only a few short months ago. The lane is Oaks and the arch under the building led onto Commercial Quay. (Rossiter Collection)

the customer. Dunne's Stores is on the site of Brien & Keating another big store of the early 1900s. The Gaelic League Hall was also in this vicinity. The Book Centre was Stones a grocery and provisions store.

Opposite this shop stood Roche's greengrocers in my youth and prior to that Doyles owned it. But it is not the potatoes that draw it to our attention. In old photographs you will notice the bottom of a sign on this building. It shows the "AL" of Theatre Royal and the reason is that an exit or entry from that theatre in High Street passed through the shop at one time.

Mr. Charles Vize had a photographer's studio here at one time. He also operated at another time from High Street. He was the projectionist at the Palace Cinema and also played in the orchestra in the days of silent movies. Contrary to popular belief orchestras accompanied the silent films rather than the stereotype piano.

We once had our own gas company in Wexford. It only closed in the 1970s. Their showroom was at number 3 South Main Street. Boggan's sold musical instruments and also operated a bus service from the premises in earlier times. Their buses departed from Anne Street.

At the top of Anne Street stood the wonderfully named Lamb House. Anne Street branches right towards the sea. It housed numerous clubs such as Masonic and Orange halls. The lower south side in 1828 had the Harbour Commissioners and Ballast

The Assembly
Rooms a century
ago. (Lawrence
Collection)

Office, which later became an Inland Revenue office. A sandy beach was excavated in 1950's at the base of the hill near the General Post Office. The GPO was built in 1894 and the Methodist Church in 1836. Number 8 Anne Street housed Anglim's, the printers of the Wexford Illustrated Almanac. The Shamrock Hotel of 1885 became the Shamrock Bar, proprietor P Meyler by 1945, it was later owned by Pierce Roche and features fictitiously in his son Billy's novel 'Tumbling Down'. Clancy's Hotel was originally a house owned by Clancy, a victualler. A room in Clancy's Hotel was let to the Temperance Club 1850. This was the first popular reading room and charged a subscription of 1d per week. Clancy's became The County Hotel when it was sold in June 1947 to the Sinnott family. In 1853 number 3a was classed as a slaughterhouse. Thomas and Mathew Boggan opened a garage in Anne Street in 1920s and ran bus fleet from Anne Street. 'Banshee' and 'Bluebird' were the names of two of the buses. They also operated a parcel delivery service along the routes. Anne Street has changed beyond recognition in recent years with government offices replacing the Shamrock and The County.

Staying on Main Street we now pass from South to North. Joyce's is number 1 South Main Street and Peter Mark is number 1 North Main Street. By Wexford logic the building in between has no number but a great history.

The Mechanics Institute, now housing Youth Train, was opened on 13 July 1849.

This is still to be seen at George's Street. It is an old boot scraper reminding us of the days of unpaved streets when the visitors needed more than a mat to remove the dirt from boots. (Rossiter Collection)

The rules included – No papers to be read at fire and no paper to be held more than 15 minutes. It offered classes, a museum and a library. The membership cost per annum was; apprentices 4/=, operatives 6/= and others 10/=. Life membership could be gained for £5 or suitable books to the value of £10. The three-storey house was purchased for £800. The original meeting to establish the institute was held in the Temperance Hall. Present were James Johnson, first editor of The People newspaper who later became a priest; Rev William Moran, Michael Hughes, George Codd, Thomas McGee who became Lieutenant Colonel Of the sixty-ninth New York Regiment and Benjamin Hughes of the Wexford Independent. Opinions on the project were sought from Charles A. Walker, Deputy Lieutenant of County Wexford and Sir Francis Le Hunte RN Both were in favour. Le Hunte who was leaving home at the time gave £100 and 1000 volumes. Books were donated by Mrs. C.S. Hall, noted for the travel book *Hall's Ireland*. Thomas Hutchinson, British Consul at Fernando Po gave 40 books plus African curiosities including a bamboo crown used by King of Bassapo in 1857; Queen Victoria gave an autographed volume and Ambrose Fortune of Wexford gave a portrait valued £50.

The Peter Mark salon is built on the entrance to Archers Lane, which connected Main Street to High Street and was marked on maps in the mid 1800s. It was covered in and reclaimed over a century ago when it became part of *The People* Newspaper offices and works. Some of the steps could still be seen when People Newspapers were on the site. It exited on to High Street through an arch just along from The Theatre Royal. Archer's Lane was the location of the Friar's chapel in the seventeenth century.

WEXFORD'S NEW CINEMA

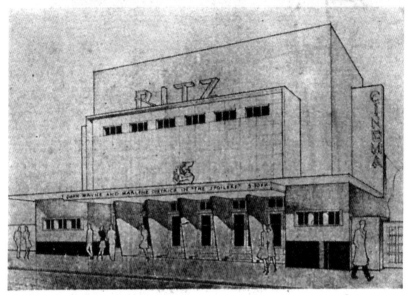

Drawing of new Super Cinema proposed to be erected in George St. Wexford. It is planned in accordance with the most modern principles of cinema design and will have a capacity of over 1,000 seats. The architects are Messrs. J. J. Robinson and R. C. Keefe, Merrion Square, Dublin.

When the Abbey cinema was first proposed this sketch appeared in the local newspapers. It reminds us of the fancy names of the cinemas and also shows how central the industry was in the middle of the 1900s that such a matter was major news.

There was a meat market with approximately 30 stalls off Archer's Lane. Clement Archer lived at Anne Street in 1834 and may have given his name to the lane.

Where the Spectra Photo shop stands was Dick Whelan's barbershop. Prior to that it was an apothecary shop for Mrs. Pierce and before her for Richards.

Moving north along Main Street the street narrows.

Hassets Chemists, held the distinction of having a telephone number of 'Wexford 1' in the 1920s. On the right another lane passes under some buildings. This is Fettett's Lane, shown on the sketch map of the town of 1812. This is how many of the old lanes towards the quay would have looked. Access to the working port was via the lanes and these were locked at night and patrolled by the harbour constables. Look at Fettett's Lane and transport yourself back. Imagine the scene each night as dusk fell and iron gates were clanged shut and locked.

Further along on the same side is the Corish Memorial Hall, named to honour Richard (Dick) Corish, Mayor of Wexford for 25 consecutive years and member of Dail Eireann until his death in 1945. In this building a school was started under the Agricultural and Technical Scheme. This school developed into the Vocational

The monument to the Redmond Family is on Redmond Square. (Rossiter Collection)

Here we can see an example of the Victorian ironwork on the platform cover of the railway station. (Rossiter Collection)

Here is street that has changed completely in thirty years. The Arts Centre, right of centre, is all that remains. Note the old ambulance and the variety of houses. (Rossiter collection)

From Cornmarket towards John's Gate Street we can observe the once thriving shops and houses. (Lawrence Collection)

School and was transferred to West Gate in 1908. The building belonged to The Irish National Foresters. The shop beside it was once the Tower Bar and before that The Oak Lounge.

Church Lane leading seaward takes its name from St Iberius Church, which it adjoins. It was originally narrow all the way from here to Custom House Quay. Here the Duke of Ely had his townhouse. It later became a Workingmen's Free Reading Rooms. It was behind St Iberius Church and can be seen in some old photographs. In September 1827 an application was made to Councilor Richards for the opening of Church Lane. In 1832, S. Howard had a factory there where they made machines for dressing flour and brushing corn. For the domestic market they produced wire riddles

135

for sifting sand or clay and wire safes, the forerunner of the refrigerator when meat was kept cool in an outside cupboard of wire sides. They also repaired umbrellas.

Opposite Church Lane and leading landward is Rowe Street, built by the Rowe Family of Ballycross. The Wesleyan Church now converted to other use but retaining its facade, was opened on 9 March 1863 with congregation of 500. The Minister of the Bethesda Church at Cornmarket reduced his Sunday services to allow people to attend, to help pay for the building. The Excise Office was located in Rowe Street in 1846 and the Inland Revenue office was at number 7 in 1875. The National League regularly met in rooms at 2 Rowe Street in 1884 and the Wexford County Board of the Gaelic Athletic Association was founded there on 21November 1885.

St Iberius Church here on North Main Street is said to be on the site of an older church originally built outside Norse market gate. The date of the present church is not clear. We have records that St Iberius was repaired in 1693. Money was requested to build a gallery in 1728. In 1831 Reverend Storey proposed Major Wilson of Roseville as churchwarden with Mr. Dance and Mr. Trigg as sidemen. The Parish Clerk was to get £20 for three services each Sunday and four in the week. Reverend Storey supplied wax candles for the reading desk and tallow candles for the congregation at a cost of £3-10-0. The vestry paid £5-11-3 for coffins for poor in 1831. This church is worth a visit with its many interesting monuments. In February 1868 the Corporation paid £5 to St Iberius Church for special pews for visiting Judges of assizes. The mayor could also use them.

Continuing north we reach The Bullring, one of the focal points of Wexford. It was called the Common Plain before bull baiting took place under a charter granted to the butchers of the town in 1609. Baiting was later transferred to John Street near the George Street junction. This spectacle of a huge beast tethered and then attacked by dogs took place at the Bullring and the hide of the animal was presented to the mayor, with the flesh being distributed to the poor of the town. In 1764 there was a courthouse with clock. It was also called Fountain Square around 1790 to 1800, when we must presume it housed a fountain. In 1833 The Bullring was stated to be 'unlit and unpaved'.

The Bullring contained a number of important buildings through the centuries. A fire engine house was located in Bullring in 1880.

The Cape of Good Hope or The Cape Bar that attracts so many photographers to snap its legend of 'bar and undertaker' was once the home of the '13 club' where members were required to consume 13 glasses of punch in quick succession. In 1831 Ambrose Fortune, in premises stated to be near Bullring, 'manufactured razors, penknives etc. to highest standard' there was also a clock and watch business. Where the bank now stands the Court of Conscience for debts under 40/= and the corporation offices were at The Tholsel in 1837 with a butter market underneath. Sixty feet of the former Shambles was purchased from Mr. Sparrow for building this Tholsel with 5 arches. At turn of the nineteenth century, 'onion women' sat on Tholsel steps twining onions and pavement selling of second hand clothes. The Fish Market was called the 'Piaze' by sailors more familiar with the Mediterranean than Dublin The Tholsel was demolished 1898.

The New Market was built in 1871. The north side buildings replaced 6 thatched houses. On 6 May 1872 it was noted in the local newspapers that the Corporation had been allowed borrow £1000 to erect the new market. Tolls at new Market included fowl 1d per basket and turkeys 1d each at Christmas.

In 1881 Laurence Murphy sold stationery next to Daly's Bakery, now the First Active office and earlier the Ritz Café. Diana Donnelly's as old rectory was the home of the Elgee family and Speranza, mother of Oscar Wilde. The house later became Pitts Coaching Inn and Morris' Hotel before being bought by Lamberts. Sheppard's statue of The Pikeman recalls the Rebellion of 1798 when the first Irish republic was declared here. The Pikeman was unveiled on Sunday 6 August 1905 by Fr Kavanagh OFM. Eleven special trains brought visitors to the event and over 20 bands attended.

Rallies such as PT Daly addressing a crowd on 3 August 1911 to say that 'dockers had won their claim and now factory workers urged to unionize', a Suffragette meeting in April 1914 and an anti vaccination protest in 1919 were regular occurrences in the Bullring. In later years victorious sporting teams were feted here. There were two air raid shelters in 1941 and an old milestone was defaced as a wartime precaution although its 64 was in Irish miles to Dublin.

The plaque to Jem Roche was unveiled on 1 October 1961. Roche is probably best known for his unsuccessful challenge for the World Heavyweight Boxing Championship against T. Burns in Dublin on St Patrick's Day, 1908 but in a career of thirty-eight fights he won twenty-two by knockouts and seven on points. One of those he knocked out was John L. Sullivan.

Leaving the Bullring and continuing north we enter what was once called Foreshore Street. The name tells it all, this was the seaside a few centuries ago.

In the intervening years the land was reclaimed and numerous businesses thrived.

Here we see the ruins of St. Patrick's Church off Patrick's Square. (Rossiter Collection)

137

Boots Chemists previously Greenacres is housed in the premises formerly occupied by Frank O'Connor's Bakery. This firm was established in 1860 and boasted some of the most modern machinery in the world. In 1889 their bread cost five pennies per four pound loaf. The fine mosaic tile floor inside the door is worthy of examination. The façade still sports the legend recalling its bakery days.

Shaw's Department Stores are on the site of Haddens, the first store in Wexford with fixed prices that opened in 1848. We now find Oaks' Lane on our right. The lane that runs parallel to Charlotte Street, one shop width to the south of it. It is now in a sad state being used as a storage area and worse. It was once worth the effort to follow the lane from North Main Street to The Quay just to view the house stretching across the arch on the quayside exit. This lane was referred to as The Old Shambles in a map of the 1840s.

Charlotte Street on the right past Oak's Lane was originally known as Custom House Lane. The name changed in the early 1800s as recorded by a Harbour Commissioner note of 1830, 'Widened the street at Old Custom House now called Charlotte Street.' In 1828 there was a request that the 'street be powder paved, new street at custom house'. At the time, it was the coach terminal, 'Shamrock Coach Co. leaves Thomas Kehoe's, Charlotte Street at 6.00 a.m. and arrives College Green, Dublin (White Horse Cellar) at 6.00 p.m. Fare 8/='. In 1917 Walter Carter of Charlotte Street was fined 6d for playing football on the street. He said that on returning from the chapel some children had kicked the ball to him and he kicked it back. The constable stated that Carter had picked up the ball, a football case filled with hay, and kicked it from Charlotte Street into Main Street. This caused inconvenience to people using the street for business or pleasure. Officially Charlotte Street is called Colbert Street.

Across Charlotte Street we find a row of shops built on the site of Walkers, an institution in Wexford of the first half of the twentieth century. For most native Wexfordians Walkers meant the smell of coffee, freshly ground. That was the aroma that permeated the store. Inside the large premises there were all the provisions one could find in the most modern supermarket. They blended their own teas. They had cellars full of wine, whiskey, stout and beer. There was a dispatch department and stabling for their horse and vans, stretching down to the quays.

Today on the narrowest point on Wexford's Main Street we find an elegant entrance to La Speranza nightclub. In the mid twentieth century the entrance was to the Coffee Shop of Whites Hotel. The hotel was founded as a coaching inn in 1779 and provided refreshment and accommodation for visitors to Wexford ever since. The building incorporated Mr. Wheelock's house where Sir Robert McCLure who discovered the North-West Passage was born. A function room within the hotel commemorated him.

William Balfe the composer lived for a time in a house opposite the hotel. His opera *Rose of Castile* was one of the first featured in the Wexford Festival Opera. The beautiful red brick building was the YMCA or Young Men's Christian Association club established in 1858. The wonderful old wooden staircase still winds its way to the second floor dividing in two on its first landing.

Number 96 North Main Street is now a fast food outlet. *The Wexford Independent* newspaper was published there in 1875 incorporating *The Wexford Journal* established in 1769.

Monck Street on the right takes its name from General Monck, Duke of Albemarle

Left side of The Faythe (Lawrence Collection)

who was granted the lands in 1658. The grant also included the rights to the ferry, which ran from the area of the Rock of Wexford to Ferrybank prior to the erection of the bridge in 1794. At that time Monck Street was called Ferryboat Lane. The Crown Hotel in Monck Street was established in 1885. In 1922 on 7 July , the first Wexford casualty of the Civil War died from a shotgun blast in Monck Street.

Strictly speaking we are now leaving North Main Street and entering Selskar Street. This area is probably the longest inhabited section of Wexford, predating the arrival of the Norsemen. Skeffington Street leads to the sea, it used to be named Ram Street after Bishop Ram. George's Street stretches landward with its many old townhouses of the gentry such as the Colcoughs and Harveys on the left. Some of the old boot scrapers of an earlier period are still evident here outside the front doors reached by several steps.

The official name is Oliver Plunkett Street. Colcoughs of Tintern had their townhouse beside entrance to the hotel. They had a theatre in the attic where visiting actors and singers performed. In 1821 a letter to Cesar Colclough on 3 November referred to a plan to open a passage or street between John Street and George Street. A cabin, occupied by Colclough's tenant was in the line of the proposed road and he was asked to have the tenant removed, as the Wexford Harbour Commissioners could not afford to re-locate him. The letter pointed out that the new road would greatly improve land value. The Christian Brothers School opened on Upper George's Street on 1 October 1853 and closed in 1971. The Constabulary Barracks was at number 5 in 1853 and was still there in 1914. It later became Miss O'Brien's Girls School. The Loreto Convent started in Wexford at 14 Lower Georges Street on Assumption Day 1866. They moved to Richmond House, then a vacant hotel, within 3 months. The first internment in Crosstown Cemetery in 1892 was a Carroll of 14 George Street. In Red Pat's field, John Duffy & Son Circus set up on 28 May 1923. Livestock auctions were held there in 1918 and Pioneer Rallies in the 1950s. The Abbey Cinema originally to be called The Ritz was built on the site.

Back on Selskar or Main Street Trimmers Lane cut east and west following the route of an ancient causeway linking Selskar Abbey to the ferry rock. The eastern lane still exists – sadly needing to be locked at night. A walk down here gives a good impression of the old town although most buildings are bricked up. Selskar Avenue on the left incorporates Trimmers Lane west. A number of houses were demolished to create the wider street.

Well Lane was previously called Bolan's Lane. In the 1800s there were 14 houses there. The name Well Lane comes from a well, later equipped with a pump in the area. In Well Lane towards the turn of the nineteenth century lived Blind Mary, the water carrier, one of the gentlest and best known characters in the town. She walked inside a barrel hoop, outside which she carried two buckets of water. She wore a short petticoat, a man's frieze coat and a deep poke bonnet. She delivered water to 'half the quality in town' until 'the newfangled water works and pipes put the pumps out of fashion'. Turning right from Selskar/North Main Street we enter another open area of importance called Redmond Square.

The square and the monument remind us of the Redmond family. We would be standing on water or marsh here but for their reclamation work. This family w s involved in politics, business, banking and land reclamation. Redmonds and their contemporaries reclaimed most of the land from Redmond Place to Carcur.

The North Railway Station or as it is officially known O'Hanrahan Station was

The Swan a century ago (Lawrence Collection)

opened on 12 August 1874. The railway originally terminated at Carcur. The station still boasts the Victorian ironwork in the platform canopy. Many people will recall the station for the machine on the platform where you paid a penny and stamped out a number of letters on a band of metal. It was also the departure point for the thousands who had to emigrate in the 1950s to find work in Britain. Michael Kelly, a former station master, reminded me that at times the crowds attending the departures were so great that a charge was made to enter the platform area.

Dunne's Stores is located on the site of Selskar Ironworks owned by Doyles. It was one of the foundries involved in the 1911 Lockout. The tile work on Dunne's tells some of our history in graphic form. That brings us to the end of the Main Street walk. A stroll round to the right will return you to Wexford Bridge.

BACK STREETS AND HIDDEN DELIGHTS

We start our next walk from Redmond Square. This time we will dart back and forth looking at the little gems of history and heritage that remain in our back streets.

Slaney Street as we head west was home to the families of lighthouse keepers at Tuskar Rock after complaints had been made by Sir Randolph Churchill about conditions for such people on the rock in winter in the 1880s. This street once formed part of the shoreline of the River Slaney.

To our right at the top of Slaney Street is Westgate. Sir Stephen Devereux built the Westgate also called Cowgate, in 1300 as part of the extended town wall. It was the entry point for goods and travellers using the ancient Coolcotts Trail. The tower had an area for collecting tolls on the ground floor with cells for detention of offenders beside it. The guards' quarters were situated above this. The town gate of Westgate was removed in 1759 along with the other four gates of the town. They were hastily re-erected at the time of the 1798 Rebellion but finally removed in 1835. What we call the tower of Westgate may not be the true gate. Recent research indicates that this tower and gate belonged to Selskar Abbey giving access to their lands outside the walled town.

We turn left at Slaney Street and enter Temperance Row. A Temperance Hall was built here in the 1800s at the time of Father Matthew's Crusade.

The dominant feature of the area is of course Selskar Abbey and church. Selskar Abbey is probably the best-known building of old Wexford but be careful, the tower is the only remnant of the abbey. The other edifice is the old Selskar Church. The original abbey was dedicated to Saint Peter and Saint Paul and by tradition was founded near the causeway used by St Ibar to reach the ferry point of departure for his monastery on Begerin, in the fifth century. The name Church of the Sepulchre was given to the abbey founded by Alexander Roche. He was a knight returning from the Crusade to the Holy Land in the time of Richard the Lionheart. On reaching Wexford he was informed that his true love had entered a convent believing him slain. He then decided to dedicate his ife to God. To that end he had an abbey erected and became its first abbot. The Abbey was used for a Synod in 1240 and a Parliament in 1463. It suffered with the Dissolution of the Monasteries in 1540 and was sacked by Cromwell in 1649. The abbey was called St Peter's of Selskar in 1240, Holy Cross in 1439 and St Sepulchre at another time. The roofless building adjoining the ancient tower today was built in 1818 at a cost of £1,400. The roof was removed in the middle of the twentieth century to avoid the cost of rates. In the 1970s the play *Murder in the Cathedral* was performed within the walls. The churchyard contains many interesting graves, including some 1798 loyalist soldiers and one belonging to the family of Thomas D'Arcy Magee, poet, scholar and politician, who left Wexford and became a founding father of the Confederation of Canada. He was assassinated in 1867.

With the historic abbey tower at our back we proceed along the street named after it, Abbey Street, showing some examples of excellent urban infill housing where once numerous small homes, forges and shops stood. The corner occupied by Pembroke House was the site of the Central Constabulary Barracks, which later became a girl's school, and than a sweet shop known as 'The Gem'. The modernised building opposite was the site of Coffey's Pawn Shop, best known in later years as Davy Tobin's', and many good suits spent their weekdays there in pre-Social Welfare days, being redeemed only for Mass on Sunday.

In the 1800s a boot factory was situated in this street. It was on the bandstand incorporated into the town wall here that the twinning of Wexford and the French Town of Coueron occurred in 1982, Wexford Mayor, Padge Reck, and Mayor of Coueron, M. Morandeau, officiated The town wall and one of its towers is visible here. A forge owned by Joe Murphy was sited beneath the tower over 100 years ago.

The wide space in front is Cornmarket. The name survives from Norman times when specific areas of the town were designated for the sale of different commodities such as meat, fish and corn. The Cornmarket of a century ago was very different from today. It had at least 20 busy shops of all descriptions. In the area now occupied by Kelly's were five separate businesses. There was a Bethesda Church, which became a theatre around 1830 with actors from London appearing on its stage. Among the other businesses of Cornmarket over the years were: The Shelbourne Hotel Michael Hanrahan's Private School, Paddy Healy's shoe repairs and Molly Mythen's pub. The latter establishment is now the 'Thomas Moore Tavern' and celebrates the name of the composer whose grandfather lived there and whose mother was born on the premises.

On being honoured by the Slaney Amateur Society, Moore referred to his grandfather as honest Tom Codd of Cornmarket'. The premises were then called The Ark and in 1835 was the headquarters of a club catering for the small shopkeepers and tradesmen of Wexford. It was a favourite haunt of nocturnal oyster eaters who could buy 100 for 10 pennies.

The dominant building in Cornmarket is the Wexford Arts Centre. In that incarnation it has provided art and entertainment for native and visitor alike since opening in 1974 but even a century before it was a place of enlightenment, amusement and leisure. It was built in 1775 as a market house. The lower windows of today were arched recesses for the traders. Inside was a magnificent ballroom and supper room. The Protestants of Wexford formed the Brunswick Club here in 1828. In 1836 the Viceroy, the Earl of Mulgrave attended a banquet here. The founder of the Methodists, John Wesley, is said to have preached here and recorded in his journal that it was one of the best public rooms he had ever spoken in. A breakfast of tea, coffee, eggs and cold meats was served here on the occasion of the re-opening of the Wesleyan Church at Rowe Street, on 10 March 1863, following renovation.

The Assembly Rooms as they were also known were popular venues for lectures such as the Gilchrist and musical evenings with entertainers such as Percy French, composer of *The Mountains of Mourne*, among other popular songs, appearing on a number of occasions. It became the headquarters of Wexford Corporation in the early part of the 1900s and was known as the Town Hall. Meetings of the town's elected representatives were sometimes interrupted by the latest dance music in their new home, as the Town Hall was for many years a popular dance hall. Indeed, the members of the Corporation even had to adjudicate on complaints, such as the dance 'The Jitterbug' which caused alarm to more serious dancers in the Town Hall in the middle of the 1900s.

Moving along this shelf of Wexford we enter Back Street, officially Mallin Street, where we can trace the old town wall along above the carpark. The Square Tower on this portion of the wall identifies it as one of the older sections. A lesson learned on the Crusades to the Holy Land, was the effectiveness of circular towers for defensive purposes, and such structures were incorporated into the walls built at a later period. The Wexford Chronicle newspaper was printed in Back Street by Mr. George Lyneall in 1782.

Crossing Rowe Street with one of our twin Catholic churches on the right and the remains of a Wesleyan Church on our left we enter High Street. This street, perhaps, more so than the Main Street, gives a feeling of the almost claustrophobic atmosphere of the narrow streets, with high buildings so common in the towns of an earlier age. On the eastern side of High Street, once called Upper Back Street, through a narrow arch, was until the 1990s part of the production area of People Newspapers Group. This group of newspaper titles grew from The People established in 1853 at 31 South Main Street by Mr. Edward Walsh. The premises were built over Archers Lane, where the Shambles or meat market with no less than 30 stalls was located in the 1880s. High Street is the home of the internationally famous Wexford Festival Opera, established in 1951

Moving south we meet Mary's Street on our right. This was called Chapel Lane and a glance up the hill quickly explains why. Filling the view of the upper part of the street is the Bell Tower of the Franciscan Chapel or Friary. At approximately the mid-point of Mary Street, the thoroughfare narrows abruptly. This was the location of Mary's Gate, called Raby's Gate for a time in the seventeenth century. To the left the car park is on the location of the old Keysar's Lane. Clarence House was situated in High Street in 1830 'on the site of Bishop Caulfield's palace'. In the same year the building was listed as a prize in a lottery. Seven houses and one garden were raffled on tickets costing three guineas each. The target figure for ticket sales was £45. When this target was not reached the draw was postponed indefinitely. Clarence Buildings were later disposed of by the more traditional methods. For a time it was owned by the Redmond family and the Sisters of Mercy lived here prior to taking over the Talbot Orphanage at Summerhill.

On the opposite side of the street the premises with a small grassed garden fronting it, is the Loch Garman Silver Bandroom. The Quakers or Society of Friends established the house in 1842, as a meeting house.

Leaving High Street we move into St Patrick's Square. Behind the high stonewalls is St Patrick's graveyard and the ruins of St Patrick's Church. The church is referred to in Chronicles dated 1534 and a vicar of St Patrick's was mentioned as early as 1420. The graveyard is the final resting place of many of the people who fought in the rebellions in 1641 and 1798. The head of Colclough of Ballytigue, who was executed on Wexford Bridge in 1798, is buried here. A portion of the old town wall and its defensive ditch is visible near the church. Adjacent to this property, was the Parochial Protestant School, which in 1824 catered for seventy-seven boys and sixty-two girls. The school was relocated in Davitt Road in the 1970s.

With St Patrick's graveyard on our right we enter Patrick's Lane. Patrick's Lane was also called Foundry Lane from Donnelley's Foundry that was located there. One claim to fame was that they made the bowls used in 'road bowling'. For many years St Patrick's Fife and Drum Band had a bandroom in the Lane. The band was commonly known as 'The Boys Band'. Their premises are now located in Lower Bride Street and the Boys' Band now includes female musicians. There was a slaughterhouse beside the lane. On a warm day you would get a very life-like feel of the streets of a medieval town. They would not be scrubbed cobbles and airy plains of Hollywood movies but bustling, crowded places without running water or drains, with animals kept close to the houses and all the related aroma.

Keeping to the lanes we cross Gibson's Lane and enter Mary's Lane. Mary's Lane is one of our finest lanes. It stretches by a meandering route that takes us past some old malt stores, a churchyard and an old oratory. The initial section is typically utilitarian lane with stores and walls. We pass Mann's Lane on our left leading to South Main Street and then round the corner into the loveliest section of Mary's Lane. Up the steps to our right is St Mary's Church and graveyard. If the gate is open it is worth exploring. This cemetery is the last resting place of many people of a military background, perhaps because of its proximity to the Military Barracks, formerly Wexford Castle situated in Barrack Street. According to the chronicles in Hore's History St Mary's was a particularly beautiful building, 'similar to but smaller and more ornamental than, Selskar Abbey and St Patrick's Church'. There was a rector of St Mary's referred to by Hore in the year 1365. This church was the parish church devastated by Cromwell. This left a period of approximately 200 years, until the opening of the town's twin churches in the mid-nineteen century, when Wexford had no official parish church.

The last parish priest of St Mary's was Dr. Ffrench who held the position from 1638 to 1651. He lived in Peter's Street and used to enter the church through his garden. After the Cromwellian occupation the bell from this church was given to a Protestant Church in Castlebridge. It was later sold as scrap, but rescued for use in Wexford dockyard. After some years of sounding shift changes at the dockyard, it was purchased and presented to the Christian Brothers for use in their monastery in Joseph Street. The annual patron day at St Mary's was on the feast of the Assumption.

The houses in this lane are excellent examples of an old town. There are dormer windows; steps leading to the door and some retain the whitewash finish. The house with the dormer windows, midway up this lane, is traditionally held to have been a mass house. From 1672 to 1691 it was forbidden by law to celebrate the Eucharist publicly. Therefore houses such as this were used. When the penal laws were relaxed the house continued as a prayer centre. In 1853 it is referred to as a chapel and schoolroom. In the 1850s the Wexford Catholic Young Men's Society was founded in this house. The society moved to larger premises at Common Quay Street in 1856 and the house returned to domestic use.

Turning right we are on Lower Bride Street. This street is mentioned in chronicles of 1650, when reference is made to a gaol belonging to a Mr. Reade situated there. It measured 30 ft. by 21 ft. and was used to house prisoners prior to Stafford's Castle being opened as a county gaol. In the present car park on the left was Wetherald Court. The property may have belonged to Catherine Wetherald who had a wine a spirits business at North Main Street. No trace remains.

From this car park we take the steps down into another car park. This incorporates Stonebridge Lane and the Ropewalk yard. A ropewalk was a common sight in most port towns. As you might imagine they were place where ropes were manufactured. They were usually long and narrow to allow for the twining of strands in the manufacturing process. The yard here stretched up behind the houses of King Street Upper. The yard became a livery stable owned by Stafford's where people travelling to town tethered their animals and carts, and also parked their bicycles. We exit the car park on to King Street and turn right. This area was prone to very serious flood into the latter years of the twentieth century. The water often reached the second floor windows.

The imposing stone buildings visible in the upper part of the street were malt stores, and are a reminder of a time when Wexford had around 30 such stores providing malting barley to small local breweries and to major breweries like Guinness in Dublin. The stores have been converted to apartments called The Pillar. This name is taken from the colloquial name of the malt stores. Legend relates that the name was derived from a tavern called 'The Golden Pillar' which stood in the vicinity some centuries ago.

We take the first left from King Street and walk into Lambert Place or as the locals call it Bunkers Hill.

Standing at the junction at the top of this hill we can see Barrack Street on our left leading back to South Main Street. This street takes its title from the military barracks standing on a hill where Wexford Castle and possibly the original Viking settlement stood. Opposite is Parnell Street. It was called New Street for a number of years. On the top right hand corner of Parnell Street stood Peter Dempsey's chipper where people from the south end of Wexford enjoyed chips, peas and pig's feet after a visit to the cinema of pub.

Behind it was Taylor's Castle one of the fine old houses built on what was once the outskirts of the town. It had gardens sweeping down towards the shore of the harbour.

To our right is Michael's Street where the seminary that preceded St Peter's College was founded in the early 1800s.

We are taking the road between Michael's and Parnell Streets. This is officially called Kevin Barry Street but most people still refer to it as Castle Hill Street from the time when it was literally the hill leading from the castle. Behind the high wall on our right is St Michael's graveyard, which served the town until St Ibar's cemetery at Crosstown, opened in 1892. Traditionally, the graveyard is on the site of the Norse church of St Michael the Archangel. It is believed that they built their church here, on high ground above the harbour and that a beacon fire was lit nightly beside the house of God. This meant that the Norse sailors first and last sight of land by day or night, was that of their church.

Our vista opens as we enter The Faythe at Swan View. In 1540 this was called FFAYGHTT STRETE The name Faythe is traced to 'faiche' an Irish word translated as a green or fair green A fair was held here on the 24 August each year. In the 1700s it was referred to as a poor area with no schools. In 1860 it was said to consist of snug cabins, housing some of the most industrious people on earth, who were mainly employed in weaving nets and spinning hemp. It was in the Faythe area that Huguenot refugees settled in the early 1700s.

Like all parts of Wexford The Faythe has a share of lanes. One leads to Cody's Well. By tradition this well is associated with the family of 'Buffalo Bill Cody', whose parents were reputed to have lived in King Street. There is no direct evidence of this but it is a good story. Directly opposite this lane was another, called Ovenhouse Lane, now identifiable by a house set back from its neighbours. At Ovenhouse Lane was one of four public bakeries of the Faythe in the early 1900s. There the locals could have their dinners, especially at Christmas, cooked at a small charge. That was in an era of houses without the gas and electric cookers of today. Swan View was probably the site of the fairs. The swan, which gives the area its title, is one of metal. Robert Stafford, a merchant, who was Mayor of Wexford, erected the fountain in 1851

The trees here are relatively new. Previously there was just a wide open square. This open area was a popular place for meetings and rallies. Most of the public meetings of the 1911 Lockout were held here including that addressed by James Connolly. In 1941 Eamon De Valera reviewed a large gathering of military volunteers, nurses and Local Defence Forces at Swan View. We leave Swan View via a short road to the left and come to the junction of Michael's Street, The Folly or Mill Road and Mulgannon or the Rocks Road. We have no shortage of alternative titles here.

At the corner of Mill Road and Mulgannon Road stood Pierces foundry on a huge site. Its official title was Mill Road Works. (Pierce's is dealt with in The Miscellany section.) Mulgannon Road was called Duncormick Road, in 1837. Proceeding up Mulgannon we encounter more malt stores. Nunn's premises at Harris's Lane are part of what remains of the vast malting industry of Wexford and the Nunn family were a major force in the business. It was in the country home of Mr. Nunn, at Castlebridge, that the seeds of the Guinness Book of Records were sown, during a discussion on the speed of the plover after a day's shooting.

The major housing developments on the left along Mulgannon Road are on the former lands of the Stafford family. Their house was Cromwell's Fort but there is little evidence that it had any connection with Oliver Cromwell. It was built in 1783 and was the Hawkes Cornock residence in 1902. The house still stands but was converted to apartments. Turning right we enter a road that did not exist thirty years ago. It was opened on land once belonging to Pierce's to connect Mulgannon to Distillery Road.

A wider view of John's Street in the early 1900s. (Lawrence Collection)

The foreground area at the base of this hill was the site of the Bishopswater Distillery. The Distillery was founded in 1827 and had a bonded warehouse cut into solid rock. It produced fine Wexford Whiskey. The company had it's own cooperage and cart-making shops. In 1912 the lands for auction on 14 Feb comprised of a boiler house, an engine room, a brewers office, an elevator room, spirit store, waterwheel, still room, corn loft and 9 distillers warehouses. There was also a grain house, gauging house, excise office, forge, grain shed, distillers house and garden, a dwelling house, managers and clerks offices, stables, coach house, harness room all within ½ mile of the town centre. The complex stretched over 12 acres giving some idea of the importance of the business in its heyday. Pierce's purchased part of the complex and they used it to build houses for their staff and used some of the land to dispose of factory waste.

We can view some of the houses at the base of the hill. This is Casa Rio. This is one of the few Wexford sites named in Latin. The translation is 'house on the river' and it is fitting. The row of houses here are quite unique if you examine them. The Bishopswater or Horse River as it is called locally flows in front of the houses. The houses at the east end are all entered by hallways built as bridges over the river and four on the western end have short bridges leading to their doors.

As we move up Casa Rio heading west a hill looms on our left. That is Avenue De Flandres. It is another Pierce's development of houses, mainly for senior management. The name is French and recalls the location of Pierce's Paris office on Rue De Flandres.

Another Pierce edifice in a sad state is 'the spout'. This lovely brick structure on the left with the legend 'aqua pura', was the source of fine spring water.

147

The housing estate of Bishops Park is built on the area once known as The Knock. Although used as a dumping ground for Pierces Foundry it was a natural adventure playground. The large trees now visible behind Bishops Park were planted by school children on Arbour Day 1952 as part of a National Trees for Ireland Project. The houses on our left are Bishopswater, an estate built in 1950. The neat bungalows on the right are another of the Pierce projects. This time the name is Alvina Brook. The houses have wonderful pillars and porches as entrances.

After Alvina Brook is Casement Terrace a relative newcomer built in the 1960s on a patch of land that previously had two or three thatched, whitewashed cottages. At Browne's Pub we turn right. We now walk through an area of Wexford that was primarily green fields a little over fifty years ago. To the right we can see the remnants of The Knock. The estate on our left is Kennedy Park named after the American President. At the top of this hill we have St Aidan's Crescent and descending towards the town we pass Whiterock View and Whitemill Road. Wolfe Tone Villas were built in 1932, Devereux Villas in 1941, St Aidan's Crescent in 1950, Whiterock View in 1938, Corish Park dates from 1955, Kennedy Park from 1970 and Liam Mellows Park from 1971.

At Jack Bailey's Pub we can look down Green Street. The street is named after John Green, who was elected mayor seven times and a champion of the idea of piped water. Into the 1950s Green Street retained its old character with lovely whitewashed houses. The lower end was called Black Cow and is now Thomas Street. Section called Black Cow had houses in a lane in 1880. St Michael's Club opened on 1 December 1963.

We turn left on to Talbot Green. This was Talbot Street in the 1900s with houses out to the footpaths. It was also called Bannister Terrace.

Mrs. Lacey had a little shop here frequented by the children going to a number of schools. Further along Pierce Roche had another small shop, later to become Bridge's shop. After that shop on the left was a field with sheds and then a row of two storey houses with walled gardens.

At the crossroads of Summerhill we continue straight ahead with the houses of Davitt Road on our left and Corry's Villas on our right. The houses of Davitt Road are built on former swampy ground. There were stories as late as the 1970s of people having seen fairies in this area. Corry's Villas are built on land donated by businessman and athlete Jim Corry. Corry's Terrace was there originally. Residents requested a name change to Waterloo Road West in 1953.

Following the line of Corry's Villas the lane to the right is called Paradise Row. No trace remains of the former houses. Thomas D'Arcy Magee's family once lived here. D'Arcy Magee was a politician, poet and author of a history of Ireland. Magee left Wexford and was one of the founders of Modern Canada. His mother and sisters are buried in Selskar Abbey churchyard.

We are now on Waterloo Road. In 1812 this street was called Methodist Row.

The house named St Aidan's on our left was the residence of Fr. James Roche as Parish Priest of Wexford in the mid-1800s. Going up the hill we have Rose Rock Terrace on our left and the convent opposite is that of the Presentation Nuns who came to Wexford in October 1818. Thomas Moore, poet and composer, visited the convent in August 1835 and after planting a tree in the grounds, entertained the sisters with some of his songs. Rounding the corner from the convent we are in Francis Street, called James Street in 1840. Here the first Wexford Praesidium of the Legion of Mary began in 1934.

This section from a picture of the early 1900s shows a nearly deserted John's Street with a cart approaching. The big tree is in John's Street graveyard. (Lawrence Collection)

The Friary Church is to the right. The Franciscan Friars are believed to have come to Wexford around 1240. They preached a gospel of penance and poverty, by example, and won a permanent place in Wexford hearts. For years this church served unofficially as the parish church of Wexford. In the early 1800s crowds gathered each Sunday afternoon under a tree in the churchyard to listen to Fr. Corrin speak. Thousands of Wexford people attended a meeting there on 10 April 1841 to hear Fr. Mathew preach a Temperance Crusade. An interesting shrine within the Church is the reliquary of St Adjutor with lifelike figure of the youthful martyr, originally presented by Pope Pius IX to Mr. Richard Devereux. The reliquary was transferred from the Devereux home to the Franciscan Church in 1883 on the death of Mr. Devereux. We now turn left onto John's Street. We are now just two streets from South Main Street and travelling parallel to it. The Church of the Immaculate Conception is on our right.

Opposite this church is Thomas Clarke Place, on the site of Duke Street or Dukes Lane. It was a street of whitewashed houses well into the last century. Perhaps the best-known character of the old Duke's Lane was John 'Buller' Wilson who had a coal yard there and made del veries by horse and cart. As we move north St Aidan's Mews guesthouse is where Hanton's Livery and Undertaking business was located at the beginning of the 1900s. At the corner of John's Gate Street and John Street is St John's Graveyard. Hidden behind whitewashed walls it is the last resting place of members of the Redmond family among others. The annual pattern was held each June on St John's Eve. The ancient Church of St John was located outside the walled town. It was granted to the Knights Hospitaller of St John in 172 and is said to have been the only medieval Wexford Church to have a steeple. The Redmond Vault is visible from the gate.

At the crossroads we pass John's Road on our left and Upper George's Street on the right. We continue up John's Street until it opens out at the junction of Wygram, Hill Street and the N25 heading west.

The double fronted house behind railings on the left was a Lying-in or Maternity Hospital. Beside was the barn in which John Moore died in 1793 following the skirmish with troops under Major Charles Vallotin. It was on the road here that the fight ng occurred and the Corporation erected the monument on the traffic island to Major Vallotin's memory shortl afterwards. The monument is believed to be the oldest in the town.

Our journey takes us right and seaward again in Hill Street. Hill Street was a street similar in character to the Faythe at the opposite end of the town a hundred years ago. It consisted of small snug cottages with well-cultivated gardens. It was called Cabbage Row at one point in its history.

In 1737 the lower end of Hill Street was the location of the Wexford County Infirmary, situated on the banks of a millstream. It is reported to have been the first such institution built in Ireland. It consisted of an infirmary and a surgeon's house. In 1837 it had thirty-five beds in ten wards and had a dispensary. Almost forty years later the numbers of beds had increased to 72 (forty-two male and thirty female). Admissions to the infirmary in 1875, except for accident cases, were on Monday, Wednesday and Friday only. Nurses in 1889 were offered twenty-five pounds per annum with rations, room, gas and coal and an indoor uniform. Many of those nursing there were members of the St John of God Order. This order of nuns was appointed permanently to the Infirmary in 1918. With the transfer of the Infirmary to the former workhouse at

Here we see thatched houses in John's Street. The posters refer to a circus on Tuesday May 24th. Note the upper storey window in the house. (Lawrence Collection)

Stoneybatter around 1923 the premises became Dr. Furlong's private nursing home. The County Council yard on the left was the location.

The County Council offices dominate the right hand side of lower Hill Street. It incorporates a Garden of Remembrance beside the last remaining cellblock of the old gaol. The entire edifice on this corner was built as the county goal in 1812 to replace one at Stonebridge. The original walls were sixteen feet to twenty feet high and enclosed fifty- eight cells, and sixteen exercise yards. Male prisoners were employed at breaking stones or on a treadmill while females were engaged in spinning, washing and knitting. Public executions were frequently carried out ere during the 1800s. Some accounts refer to the niche above the main gate at Westgate, where a statue of St Brigid once stood, as the execution spot. However this sounds more like the stuff of legend and films. In the Wexford Directory of 1878 there is a story of John Redmond and Nicholas Jackman being executed for the murder of three people and it relates that they died on a wooden gallows erected on the gaol green in March 1833.

Public executions continued until 1860. The building ceased to be the county gaol n the early years of the twentieth century. The buildings then came under the management of the Sisters of St John of God as St Brigid's Home for Inebriates. But even while used for that purpose it became necessary to use the premises to house prisoners again at the time of the 1916 Rising and to accommodate victims of the great influenza epidemic in 1918. During the Civil War it was used as a jail by the National Army and on 13 March 1923, the first Wexford executions of that war took place here. Those who died were James Parle, Patrick Hogan and John Creane, who had been found guilty of possessing arms at Horetown, Taghmon a few days before. Today the old gaol is the County Council Headquarters as well as containing Wexford Courthouse.

Directly opposite the end of Hill Street on Spawell Road, which is named after a spa or well with curative powers popular in the sixteenth and seventeenth centuries, is Glena Terrace. This beautiful row of red brick houses was built by a female building contractor named O'Connor on part of the land of Wellington Cottage, now renamed Ardara.

Rounding the County council offices we pass yet another new street. This is 1798 Street opened only a few years ago. It is built on Fortview residence and grounds. The residence was so named because the fort at Rosslare was visible from here. The house was of note principally because documents and records were stored there during the Civil War to protect them from destruct on by opposing forces. Beside the County Council Buildings stands Wexford Vocational College. It retains the older building at the kerb. This was once a private residence owned by the Harvey family. Later the house was divided in two with George Jacobs residing in one portion and the County Club occupying the other. It was known as Spawell House.

The West Gate Bar opposite the West Gate Yard was in 1856 the site of McDonnell's, Westgate Hotel. In the intervening years it has had various owners, Walpole, Ryan and McCabe. Beside these buildings, a restaurant is located in a former grain store. The steep hill beside the restaurant was Kaat's Lane and led to the shipyard of Anthony Van Kaat who came to Wexford from the Netherlands and built ships for the Confederate Navy between 1641 and 1649. After Cromwell had taken the town, the local Catholics were transported, some to Barbados from this quay. The strand across the Slaney from here is often called Kaat's Strand. With the reclamation work of last century the waters edge has been far removed from the old Kaat's Quay.

Let's turn into Westgate with its interpretive centre where you could rest and hear more about our past or go into the graveyard of Selskar Abbey. Walking through the old gate under the tower we can see the recesses similar to those where watchmen waited at the town gates 700 years ago to close the gates at dusk.

We are now outside the old Norman town of Wexford. Turning left we are on George's Street. We stroll down this street where the gentry lived. Directly in front on Main Street is a house whose rent was donated to Wexford Corporation by the writer George Bernard Shaw towards civic works.

We cross Selskar Street and enter Trimmers Lane West to bring us to the harbour.

Exiting Trimmers Lane we face the goods yard and to the right Wexford Bridge where our trip back in time began.

BIBLIOGRAPHY

Berney (editor) – Centenary Record (1956)

Browne – County Wexford Connections (1985)

Browne & Wickham – Lewis's Wexford (1983)

Cambrensis – The Historical Works, H.G. Bohn, London (1863)

Echo Newspaper (various)

Enright – Men of Iron, WCTU (1987)

Forde (editor) – In Ibar's Footsteps, Kara Publications (2005)

Free Press Newspaper (various)

Furlong & Hayes – Wexford in the Rare Ould Times-Volumes 1, 2 & 3

Grannell – the Franciscans in Wexford (1975)

Griffith Valuation

Griffiths Chronicles

Hore – History of the Town and County of Wexford (1906)

Jenkins – Retailing in Wexford 1930-1990 (1996)

Journals of the Wexford Historical Society

Kehoe – Wexford Its Street & People (no date)

People Newspaper (various)

Pigot's Directory (1824)

Ranson – Songs of the Wexford Coast (1975 reprint)

Reck – Wexford a Municipal History, Mulgannon Publications (1987)

Roche, Rossiter, Hurley & Hayes – Walk Wexford Ways (1986)

Rossiter – Wexford May 1917, WCTU (1992)

Rossiter – Wexford Port, a history, WCTU (1989)

Rossiter, Hurley, Roche & Hayes, WHP (1994)

Ruddock & Kloss – Unending Worship, (1997)

Wexford Directory (1875 & 1878)

Wexford Historical Society Journals (various)